# EPPING FOREST

# EPPING FOREST

*Its History and Wildlife*

ALFRED LEUTSCHER

## DAVID & CHARLES
NEWTON ABBOT  LONDON  NORTH POMFRET (VT) VANCOUVER

ISBN 0 7153 6662 9

Set in 11 on 13pt Imprint and printed in
Great Britain by Latimer Trend & Company Ltd Plymouth
for David & Charles (Holdings) Limited
South Devon House  Newton Abbot  Devon

Published in the United States of America
by David & Charles Inc  North Pomfret
Vermont 05053 USA

Published in Canada by Douglas David & Charles Limited
3645 McKechnie Drive  West Vancouver BC

# CONTENTS

# LIST OF ILLUSTRATIONS

# INTRODUCTION

On 8 August 1878 the Epping Forest Act was passed so that some 5,500 acres of woodland and open spaces, part of the former royal hunting Forest of Essex, and one-time realm of the East Saxons, might be preserved as a pleasure ground for the people of London to enjoy. The events which slowly led up to this important Act go back far into the past. In tracing the fascinating story of this famous forest which has seen so much of England's history, signs of those earlier times can still be seen during a present-day ramble.

Travelling through the endless rows of shops, houses and factories of London's East End, we arrive eventually on the doorstep of the Forest by following one of the main roads leading out in a north-easterly direction. Suddenly, at Forest Gate, Leytonstone, Walthamstow or Chingford, there are open spaces, and we step on to the grass of Wanstead Flats or Chingford Plain.

There are no hedges or fences to bar the way, for the Forest boundary, although well defined by law, has no enclosure. Almost at once we may see the curious sight of free, untethered cattle quietly cropping the grass, or leisurely crossing the road to hold up the busy traffic. Entering a wood, we notice the odd shape of the oak, beech or hornbeam trees which have suffered from the lopper's axe. Such is the evidence of the ancient commoners' rights—the 'right of lopwood' and the 'right of common of pasture'. But there is more to the Forest story than this. For centuries the monarchs and their favoured subjects used it to

9

enjoy the sport of venerie—the hunting of the deer. Maybe farther north beyond Loughton and Chingford, where the Forest closes in, we may catch a glimpse of a shy, dark-coloured fallow deer as it slips away between the holly. It is the descendant of some distant ancestor which may have been hunted by a Stuart, Plantaganet or even a Norman king some 700 years ago. Stand on the ramparts of the ancient earthworks romantically associated with Queen Boadicea. This goes back even farther, before there was British history.

Apart from these historic glimpses, there is the present-day Forest and its wildlife to look for and enjoy. Today's hunter takes with him a camera in place of a gun. By virtue of the Act, the ground and trees are now preserved from encroachment, lopping and hunting, and so have become a sanctuary for plant and beast within the ever-sounding murmur of London's heartbeat. The bustling City and its corporation who are the Forest's guardians are but 5 miles from where we can commence our walk.

From Forest Gate to Epping town we can travel on Forest soil for some 10 miles, with roads to cross only here and there. Choose a spring day to admire the crab-apple blossom, a fruit tree once planted to provide the deer with food. Sit quietly one evening in May and listen to the nightingale behind the Connaught Water, named after the first Forest ranger appointed by Queen Victoria, or wait patiently at dusk 'somewhere in Monk Wood' to see old brock emerge from his sett, as he did long before the Romans came.

In a glade we come across the shy adder, a ribbon of beauty rather than the dangerous serpent it is made out to be, for it will not attack but seeks refuge beneath the thorn bush nearby. Choose an autumn day when the sun breaks through the morning mist, and revel in the glories of colour, the red of the hawberry, bronze of beech leaf and yellow-gold of toadstool. In winter snow, follow the spoor of the wandering fox to learn more of his nightly secrets. These are but a few of the things which a discerning rambler may see on a visit to London's Forest. They are glimpses of its history and its natural history.

## Introduction

In the following pages the story of the Forest will be told yet again, as it has been many times by others, if only to remind us of the debt we owe to the few farsighted people who stepped in to save it from total destruction. There is also the need to understand the background to any countryside, if one is to study its wildlife. Epping Forest is, odd as this may seem, an artificial place where man's presence has been felt for centuries, as it still is. This is bound to have an affect on the wildlife. In the second half of this book, which deals with the Forest's natural history, repeated reference will be made to the influence of historic events, such as lopping, gravel digging, hunting and so on, which have left their mark on the present-day habitats.

The Forest story is in four parts punctuated by three dates— 1066, the arrival of a dictator; 1649, the beheading of a king; and 1878, the passing of an Act of Parliament. All these 2,000 years of history record the use made of land by its human occupants. From the ancient Forest of Essex to the modern Epping Forest, the story has passed through various stages—savage, hunting, utilitarian. We are now in a fourth stage, an aesthetic period. It may be that, in the light of today's pressure on the land, there is a fifth and final stage yet to come. This is discussed in the Epilogue.

# I

# A FOREST STORY

The extent of forests in a country reflects the progress of the nation. Their history is marked by three great epochs—savage, sporting and utilitarian, corresponding to man's relation to the forest and its denizens.

P. J. S. PERCEVAL. *London's Forest*

### THE SAVAGE FOREST (500 BC–AD 1066)

Some 10,000 years ago Britain began to emerge from the grip of the Ice Age. The great ice sheet had penetrated as far south as Essex, below which there lay a wind- and snow-swept arctic waste of moss and lichen-covered ridges rising among patches of stunted birch and willow. This bleak tundra was the home of mammoth, reindeer, arctic fox and Palaeolithic man.

As the vast ice field and glaciers retreated to the north, they were followed by the reindeer and the willow trees, whose place was taken by pine forests and red deer as the climate warmed. Melt waters poured out of the valleys and a slow rise in sea level with some land subsidence brought about an event of far-reaching consequences to the land. About 8,000 years ago the final breach was made by the sea, severing Britain from the Continent at the Straits of Dover. We became an island and this was to have two results. Firstly, the boreal climate associated with northern countries gave way to milder maritime weather which we enjoy, or perhaps suffer from, today. Secondly, the pine moved north in the wake of the ice, and oak forests covered the heavy London clay of the Thames basin and slopes.

13

## A Forest Story

There is only scanty evidence of human occupation in these deep woodlands in prehistoric times. The first invaders to come by boat were the late Stone Age farmers of the Neolithic Period who preferred the higher and more fertile chalk downlands to the north and south of the forest areas. Here they settled in communities to rear their farm stock and grow their crops. The downlands of Britain were probably the first places in the country to lose their trees, and have remained as farmland ever since. In the central forest zone of the Thames basin the earliest sign of any settled community is an early Iron Age village. During the building of the Lea Valley reservoirs near Walthamstow, the site of an old British encampment was uncovered, and dates back to around 500 BC. At about that time Celtic invaders from western Europe were arriving in Britain. These were the peaceful farmers of the Hallstadt culture called the Trinobantes, named after a locality in Austria. They were slowly being pushed towards the Atlantic coast by a more militant race of the La Tène culture, who were also to follow across to Britain from France. Whereas the La Tène warriors settled more in the south-east, a party of Hallstadt immigrants penetrated the Thames and turned up the Lea Valley. Here they built their homes as pile dwellings in the fertile marshes, surrounded by a stockade to protect themselves and their cattle from the wild beasts. The lush meadow grass provided pasture for their animals, and reeds for thatch were gathered from the marsh. On the valley slopes the farmers terraced the soil for growing their crops. Fish, water fowl and beaver were caught from the river, and larger game such as boar, bear and deer were taken from the forested heights on occasional forays. From here, too, could be gathered timber and fruit from the trees. However, as a farming folk rather than a hunting tribe, these forest settlers probably avoided the deep and dark woods as much as possible, for here was the domain of dangerous beasts and demons.

Even so, there is strong evidence, both from dating and siting, to think that the two hill-camps inside the Forest, were linked with the village down in the valley. The larger of the two well-preserved forts, called Ambresbury Banks, lies just to the south of Epping town and is easily seen from the main London road. A second, smaller camp, called Loughton, or Cowper's Camp, is named after its discoverer Mr Cowper-Temple, one of the founders of the Commons Preservation Society which played a valuable role in saving the Forest (see page 40). It lies deep inside Monk Wood, on high ground above Loughton. Both camps are of similar build, on hill-tops and constructed around natural springs. What are such earthworks doing in these places, hidden among the trees? Who built them and what were they used for? Questions like these can only be answered by excavation, since this is part of prehistory.

In 1881-2 the first dig was carried out by the Essex Field Club, under the guidance of General Pitt-Rivers, a leading antiquarian of his day. One certain fact emerged from this. The camps are definitely not of Roman origin since the flimsy fragments of pottery, flint chippings, pot-boilers and other artifacts are of a British character. Also, the ramparts follow the contours of the ground, and do not conform to the more rigid geometrical pattern of a Roman fort. In each camp the original rampart and the V-shaped outer ditch, or fosse, appear to have been 10ft tall and correspondingly deep. Pitt-Rivers' conclusion was that the evidence found at the two camps was sufficient to 'identify the camps as pre-Roman, and probably of a very early period'. This view was confirmed in 1926-7 when the bank and ditch was sectioned under the leadership of Mr Hazzledine Warren, although no firm date was given.

More recently, in 1956 and 1958, further sections were made at both camps during courses given by the London University Extra-mural Department, held at the Essex Further Education Centre of Wansfell, near Theydon Bois. This time a firmer date of about 500 years BC was arrived at and this ties up with the Lea Valley settlement already mentioned. The conclusion drawn as to the actual purpose of these camps is uncertain, but one comment—which was not meant to be facetious—is that they were the prehistoric equivalent of air-raid shelters. They were not in permanent occupation, but could have been used at temporary hill-top retreats, easily reached by means of the side valleys. Here the valley farmers could have hidden with their families and cattle during times of danger. Carts and chariots were already in use, and this would mean trackways. Where one tribe had penetrated, another, with intent to raid, could follow.

Half a millennium was to pass before man made his second impact on our Forest story; this is now recorded for us in the first pages of British history. Caesar had much to write about during his reconnaissance trips to Britain, both of the people he met and the countryside he traversed. By then, in 55 BC, the Belgic tribes, also from Europe, were firmly settled in the area. From them was to arise a proud and militant leader of the Icini, the first British queen, Boudicca—or Boadicea, as we usually spell her name. She has long been linked with the Epping hill camp, although we now know that it was erected long before her reign.

The first permanent settlement of the Romans was built in AD 43, on the north bank of the river Thames, at a position which in those days was probably the highest tidal reach and the lowest fording place. Some say this was on the site of the former Celtic centre of Lyndin. In the reign of Emperor Claudius his general, Aulus Plautius, built a supply port and garrison from which forced marches by his legionaries could be made to the subsidiary garrisons at Colchester (Camulodunum) and St Albans (Verulamium). So began an uneasy occupation which was to last for nearly 400 years and during which the Romans built their walled city of Augusta on the two hill-tops known today as Tower Hill and Ludgate Hill. One was later to support a fortress—the Tower, and the other a place of religious teaching —St Paul's. The Wallbrook, now a road, flowed in between.

Along the straight roads through the Forest, connecting the city with Colchester and St Albans, British forces, using guerilla tactics, harried the Roman columns with chariot and spear against sword and armour. These early pages of British history, so beloved by every schoolboy, bring us back to the Forest

*Page 17*   Winter silence in the heart of Monk Wood

*Page 18*  Gateway and tower of Waltham Abbey, built by Harold

slopes, to a place described by the historian Tacitus as 'a position approached by a narrow defile, closed in at the rear by a forest'. Somewhere, in the Forest area, it is believed, the final battle was waged between Briton and Roman. Having avenged the insults heaped upon her by the invaders, Boadicea had taken revenge by sacking Colchester and St Albans, then marched upon London. In retaliation the Roman general Suetonius drove the queen's forces back into the Forest and so to her defeat along the slopes of Epping Upland. Close by, the tragic queen took her life with poison, it is said, on the banks of the tiny Cobbin brook, which empties into Izaak Walton's favourite river Lea. So, in AD 61, a forest queen passed into history. Today, in stone effigy, she and her two daughters hurl defiance from their chariot at the Mother of Parliaments. The statue stands at the north end of Westminster bridge in the shadow of Big Ben.

On the withdrawal of the Romans after holding a police state for 400 years, Forest history becomes obscure during the Dark Ages which followed. Presumably, as before, life went on among the Anglo-Romans but with less supervision from a central power. Instead, the country slowly split into minor kingdoms divided between chiefs and overlords whose power must have shifted between separate loyalties. By Anglo-Saxon times the more-or-less settled kingdoms were receiving names; that of the East Saxons, called Essex, covers the area we are interested in. At one time this was joined with the Mid Saxon kingdom of Middlesex to form one unit.

Farming went on as before in an agricultural community living under the tribal system. Surrounding each little community in a thinly scattered population were pieces of cultivated land treated as common property. That is, each member of the village, or 'vill', was entitled to a piece so as to contribute his share of food to the common store. Under an open-field system, one-acre strips were marked out with banks of turf or temporary fences of deadwood. It is quite possible that some of the Essex hedgerows still standing today originated from this method of demarkation. A fresh branch used as a stake can easily strike root and so become a bush. The hawthorn (from the Anglo-Saxon *haga*, a hedge) is particularly suited to this treatment. Cultivated one year, and put to fallow the next, this open land and its produce was shared by the villagers. Then, on each Lammas Day (1 August), the fences were removed and the cattle allowed to pasture on the fallow ground until the next seed time, that is, between haymaking and when the fields were again 'shut up' for the next crop seeding. The only private land was that owned by the chieftain, whose demesne was his own property. This was a kind of forerunner to the estate of the manor lord in later years. All the open wasteland outside the cultivated areas was used as permanent pasture for cattle and as acorn ground for pigs, also for the hunting of game. In those days the hunting was done more out of necessity to obtain meat and clothing than for pleasure.

This, in essence, was the state of the land and its use during the days before the Crown and Church took control. Land belonged to the people and not to authority; the important distinction in the way in which the countryside was used and shared should be borne in mind when we come shortly to the Norman regime.

THE HUNTING FOREST (1066–1649)

The Great Forest of Essex, known as Waltham Forest since the thirteenth century, was to become the setting for a highly colourful age of pleasure and pageantry, in so far as the favoured few were concerned. This included the Crown, the Church and certain high dignitaries in the king's favour. Even prior to the Norman occupation certain areas of land were already in the possession of the king and known as the King's Woods, or Sylvae Regis. The Danish and Anglo-Saxon kings exercised a right to claim pieces of common land for private use, implying that this was for the good of the state since the land would now come under royal charter. This was the so-called boc-land, or folk-land, and could be used at the king's pleasure for hunting.

This somewhat dictatorial attitude was received by the common people with misgivings, as it tended to restrict their own use of the land. Canute the Dane sat at Winchester with his nobles to formulate and pass the first laws to protect the deer. His standard-bearer, Tovi, much impressed with the abundance of game, built a special hunting lodge at Waltham on the Forest outskirts. For centuries afterwards this great centre, in which Harold built his church, was to be the meeting place for many a sovereign seeking pleasure and rest from the cares of state. As the sixteenth-century historian Camden wrote of the district, 'Near the Ley spreads out a chase of vast extent, full of game, the largest and fattest in the Kingdom.'

King Alfred the Saxon was no doubt also a keen huntsman but is better known for his exploits in protecting his kingdom and in repelling the invading Danes. One incident of local interest may be mentioned here. The Danes appear to have sailed out of the Thames and into the Lea to reach as far as Hertford. The anxious citizens of London turned to their monarch for aid, so Alfred followed in their wake and 'by fortune Kinge Alfred passinge by espied that the channel of the river might in such sorte be weakened, that they should want water to return with their shippes; he caused therefore the water to be abated by two great trenches and setting the Londoners upon them, he made them batteil'. The Danes 'forsooke all and left their shippes as a prey to the Londoners, who breaking some and burning others, conveyed the rest to London'.

Methods of catching animals for food in Saxon days included the use of nets, traps, bows and dogs. The Saxon huntsman would 'take harts, boars, Dere and Roes, and sometimes hares. I braid the nets and set them in a convenient place and set on my hounds that they may pursue the beasts of chase until they come unexpected to the nets, and so became entangled in them, and I slay them in the nets'. Such a royal huntsman had a pleasant task. In return for the kill which went to the king, the huntsman was fed and clothed, and might even be rewarded with some trinket, even a horse, for his devotion and skill. Royal interest in hunting was beginning to make itself felt, and all except the favoured church officials and the Thanes were subject to the hunting laws. Hunting by the Crown is first recorded in the tenth century by the Abbot Aelfric.

It was with the arrival of the French that the word 'forest' came into use in the English language. One of Duke William's first acts was to claim legal ownership of the entire realm, and to select here and there those bits of countryside most favoured by wild deer, so that he might pursue his favourite pastime of hunting, or venerie. It is written that he 'loved the Great Game as if he had been their father'. This old pursuit brought with it a whole new vocabulary of words, as well as a new attitude towards the land. To understand this, it is necessary to appreciate the precise meaning of the word 'forest'. Today it is usually applied to a tree-covered landscape, and spoken of as a coniferous forest, a deciduous forest or a tropical rain forest, according to the type of tree and climate. Originally, however, the word appeared in a legal phrase 'forestem sylvam', but has long since been taken out of context. Derived from the Norman 'foris' meaning 'outside' or 'without', and from the Latin 'sylva', a wood or park, we come to the phrase 'outside the wood'. A wood or park in its original state was a piece of privately owned land surrounding some property, such as a palace, a baronial castle, a monastery, or a manor house. Such land was usually enclosed. Any land 'outside the wood' was open waste, and called the forest land. An alternative but less likely origin of 'forest' might have been the Norman 'feresta' from the Latin 'ferarum statio', a habitation for wild beasts. Such land was usually tree covered, since the favoured game of the Norman huntsman were deer, and these are woodland animals. Whatever its original meaning a forest was laid down by royal charter as Crown property and covered by certain laws. In Canute's time there was a certain code of procedure in the management of such Crown land, but not until the Normans took over was this turned to more personal advantage. The laws were embodied in the Carta de Foresta, or Lawes Forrest, so as to protect the forest land and its deer and trees. This automatically protected the sovereign's 'Kingely right to vert and venison' (trees and deer). To protect such rights a whole army of officials came into being and a complicated legal machinery was set in motion. Its function was to regulate the activities of the commoners, who claimed certain rights, and at the same to give protection to the deer and other game. It is in this situation that we come to the very heart of the whole question as to who owned what land, and who had a right to do this or that.

By definition a piece of common land is ground to which there is free access for the public and around which there are no barriers. It is the land of the people, so to speak, even though it may be privately owned. Ancient charter mentions certain 'common woods, marshes and meadows for sheep, swine and other animals to feed on'. The ancient vills were usually situated within easy access of such commonable land. The pastures where cattle used to feed, and still do in Epping Forest, were sometimes called lawns. These were the open spaces and glades between the wooded areas, such as Balmer Lawn, just outside Brockenhurst in the New Forest. To prevent cattle straying on to the highway, gateways or hatches were sometimes erected, as at Chingford Hatch in Epping Forest.

This free range of cattle and pigs, as well as other domestic stock, such as hens, ducks, geese, goats and sheep, was the normally accepted practice of the village communities before the Crown took a hand, and it was a quite natural desire to want to retain this birthright. In the early days the vested interests of the Crown, also that of private landowners, did not clash too severely with the ancient freedom of the commoners and their beasts. There was enough space for all to share, and the early Anglo-Saxon farmers gave little thought to any need for a claim to land use, since this did not arise. Since the dawn of farming, the common use of land as an accepted birthright has been handed down through each generation.

Even during the early Norman regime, the land covered by Waltham Forest was still thinly populated. Fisher quotes the following from the famous Domesday Book of 1086: '2 priests,

513 villeins, 451 bordarii, 58 serfs and 18 freemen'. This was mainly for the manors of Barking and Waltham, the two seats of the great abbeys, and for East Ham and Walthamstow near by London. Even doubling these figures would still give a thin spread of humanity. As settlements increased and spread, it became necessary to have some kind of law and order so as to make and maintain adjustments to the social management of land. As more and more waste land was appropriated, either by squatting or by plunder, or as gifts from the Crown, it became identified with certain groups of people, and no longer as common property. As this private ownership increased, so did the ancient rights of commoners begin to show their limitations.

It was when the Norman dictator exerted his authority by placing the land under royal ownership that the whole question of who had the right to do this or that came to a head. To have taken away the rights of the commoners in those early days before industry and overseas trade would have been like committing national suicide. England was mainly a pastoral and farming community, and the country's life-blood was nourished by its farm produce. Indeed, the farming stock in each village community existed long before the Normans arrived, so that a conqueror's will had to be imposed on a deep-rooted way of life already long in existence. In the circumstances the best approach was a compromise. Those areas which were afforested, in the legal sense, would come under the hunting laws. At the same time the commoners would be allowed to carry on with their ancient practice of commonage and lopping. However, various officials were now brought in to control the cattle, to brand them, supervise the lopping, watch for illegal enclosure, patrol the forest area, officiate at court, and so on. It is interesting to note that, in many places, the boundaries of the afforested land actually cut across some of the old vills, implying that these settlements existed long before the royal forests were created. In Domesday Book the vills within the Waltham Forest boundaries are listed, but the Royal Forest, as such, is not even mentioned. One of these vills, the Manor of Waltham founded by Tovi in

Canute's day, is even recorded by date. Fisher suggests from this that no forest laws could have existed before the Conquest. It was by this means that the commoners living within the forest boundaries could carry on with their daily activities provided that they respected the laws. Meanwhile the Crown and a chosen few could pursue their pleasures of hunting.

From time to time the Crown enforced the law with severity, at other times with laxity. Some sovereigns, in order to extend their authority over more of the land and also to swell the royal coffers by imposing rentals, would extend the boundaries of the Forest. At one time England was divided into two great forest areas, with the Trent and Severn as a dividing line. In each major forest, under a king's justice, there was a warden appointed for each minor forest, such as Waltham Forest. Under his administration a host of officials managed the various duties and enforced the law. The more localised verderers, four to each forest, were people of substance such as knights and resident landlords. They attended the forest courts and generally saw to forest business. The foresters, equivalent to today's gamekeepers, patrolled their beats to keep law and order. At one time they were unpaid and had to earn their keep by the levy of dues and taxes on the villagers. They even paid the forest warden for their job, which could give them a profitable living. Extortion of this kind often led to abuse, especially when it was carried out on commonable land where rights existed free of charge. Fisher quotes a case under the ruling of the Select Pleas, to which a commoner could turn in court in order to air a grievance. In this instance the men of Somerset in 1277 complained to the court of a forester who collected corn from them as his due, made it into ale, then forced the same people to buy it back. In other cases, lambs and piglets were confiscated, and trees felled for fuel.

These kinds of iniquities were more resented by the villagers than the official limitations on hunting and woodcutting imposed by Forest law. Consequently there were often demands for a new perambulation of the Forest boundaries, so as to free land from a law which at the same time was being abused by the officials. An

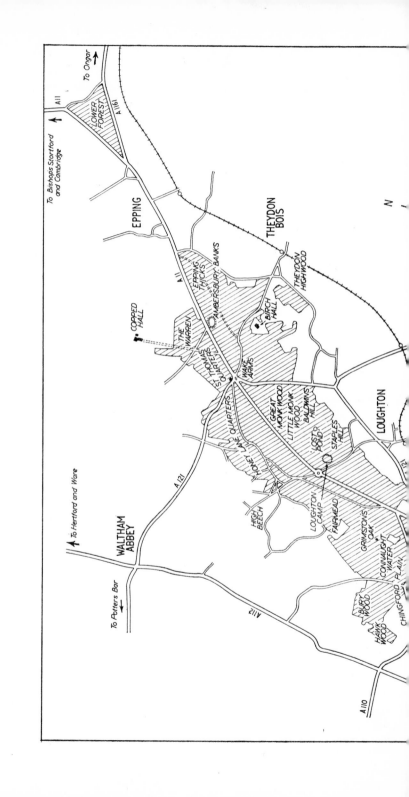

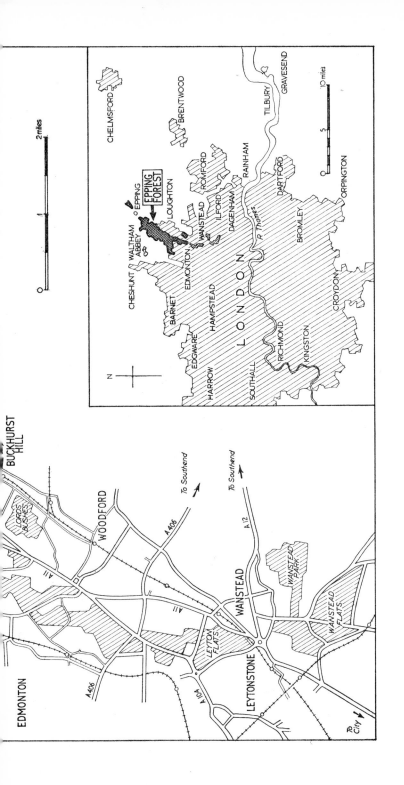

interesting example of the kind of legal tangle which could arise over the rights of the Crown and those of the commoner occurred in the ancient manor of Havering, which was at one time Crown demesne. It was also part of the Hundred of Becontree in the time of Edward I, and so part of the Royal Forest included within the perambulation of 1301. His son, Edward II, gave this manor as dowry to his consort Queen Isabella in 1323, with the power to nominate her own officials. By this means Havering became a liberty separated from Becontree, yet the Crown still claimed it in 1603 when James I took the throne. This meant that the Forest courts once more had jurisdiction over the manor. The Havering people, as inhabitants and tenants, protested that they had always enjoyed the right of commonage and had even paid for the privilege, but had never been required to appear before any Forest court. They even had their own ranger. This tangle was finally resolved by the 1641 perambulation when Havering was separated from the Forest (see page 32). This kind of dispute between commoner and authority is a foretaste of what was to come as a climax to the Epping Forest story in the nineteenth century (see page 41). The Hundred of Becontree included West Ham, East Ham, Waltham, Leyton and Ilford; it was named after the beacon which burned on Windmill Hill at Woodford in order to call the Forest knights to arms in defence of England.

By the time of John's reign, the grievances of the people against the severity of the forest laws, started by Canute the Dane and upheld by William and Rufus, were no longer tolerated. This led to the limitation of forest land to what became known as the Forest of Waltham (first mentioned by name in 1205: 'foresta nostra prope Waltham'). Large tracts had previously been annexed by Henry II and brought under Forest law. Actually, much of the land even then was vested in the powerful religious bodies of Waltham and Barking, to which the Crown only held the sporting rights. On many occasions land was given away as a royal favour for services rendered. In return the owners and occupants were expected to offer hospitality to the monarch on the occasions of his visits and hunting trips, by providing lodging and food for his royal person, his huntsmen, dogs and hawks. These became known as the loen, or loan, lands of which the manors of Barking and Waltham were particularly favoured, as were the abbeys themselves. Used not only as seats of learning and religious instruction, they provided many an hospitable occasion for royal revelry.

Originally the Great Forest of the East Saxons became two when the smaller kingdom of the Middle Saxons was created. The river Lea separated these two, as it does today, and also became the boundary of their respective forests. The parent forest became for the most part a royal demesne of the Saxon kings who loved their sport. It is handed down that the seven petty monarchs would join together for the chase and later refresh themselves and their mounts by the stream called the Seven Kings Water. It was conveniently situated close by the great abbey of Barking founded by Erkenwald, King of East Anglia and also spiritual head of St Paul's as its bishop. It was he who, no doubt, helped to cement the friendship between the various Saxon kingdoms in the shared pleasures of hunting.

All this was to be taken in conquest by the Conqueror, and handed on to Rufus. Henry I continued the sport and spoke of retaining 'in my hands all forests in the manner as they were held by my father'. He even extended the boundaries to the very corners of Essex. Next, Stephen, in order to ingratiate himself with his people, promised to restore that which his father had annexed, and gave it back to the Church and former owners. The forest which was held by William Rufus he retained. Henry II chose to ignore this disafforestation by Stephen and restored the old forest boundaries. In this, Richard I and John followed suit. By then the oppression created by the forest laws had reached such a pitch that even the high-ranking nobles were in revolt.

With the signing of the famous Magna Carta, extorted from John by his rebellious barons, severe restrictions were made on forest territory, as well as an easing of punishment. The forming of the Carta de Foresta, a kind of legal forest code, forced Henry

III to restore all the lands originally afforested by his great-grandfather, Henry II. The Church also did much to lighten the commoners' burdens. Rights of ploughing and pannage (pig feeding on acorns) were restored, but more important, perhaps, was the revision of punishments.

> No man shall henceforth lose either life or member for killing our Deer. But if any man be taken and convicted for taking our Venison, he shall make a grievous fine, if he have anything whereof; and if he have nothing to lose, he shall be imprisoned a Year and a Day; and after the Year and Day expireth, if he can find sufficient sureties, he shall be delivered; and if not he shall adjure the realm of England.

In order to carry out a perambulation, the forest boundaries were reviewed by 'good and lawful men' from time to time, who should see to it that any wood outside his own demesne should be disafforested if it cause any hurt to the owner or occupier. Forest boundaries were identified by natural landmarks such as hills, rivers, trees, occasional buildings and boundary stones. They were 'meered and bounded with unremoveable marks, meeres and boundaries'.

The particular perambulation made in 1225 in the reign of Henry III, and in accordance with the Carta de Foresta, reads as follows: 'a perambulation made by twelve lawful knights . . . according to the tenor of our Charter of Forest liberties granted to our good men of England . . .' It goes on to give the boundary limits of the King's Forest. This was not to the king's liking, so in one audacious act he simply cancelled the Charter with a stroke of his pen, and all previous disafforested land in the Charter was restored to the Forest and once again covered most of Essex. In 1277 Edward I proclaimed the extent of his forest as 'the Forrest of the lord and King in the county of Essex is included in meeres and bounds from the Bridge of Stratford unto the Bridge of Cattywad [this crossed the river Stour at Manningtree] in length, and in breadth from the Thames unto the King's highway which is called Stanestreet'. Finally, in 1300, Edward was forced to restore the original boundaries made during the 1225 perambulation.

Some centuries later, Charles I also attempted to increase the Royal Forest boundaries, more with the intention of extorting fines and dues from those whose land now fell within the new boundaries. Those who owned houses or property on Forest soil were fined for having encroached, and even had to forfeit property if they could not pay. Those with sufficient money could pay to have their property removed from forest law. In Essex alone, in 1640, some £20,000 was raised in this manner. However, due to strong Commonwealth sympathies in Essex during the Civil War, the king felt obliged to proclaim, with his tongue in his cheek no doubt, that 'His Majestie, understanding that Forest laws are grievous to subjects of his kingdom, out of his grace and goodness to his people, is willing that the Bounds be reduced to the same conditions as before'.

This continuous juggling with Forest land by successive monarchs, according to the disposition or maybe for economic needs or just greed, is one of the strong features of the Forest story, time and again giving rise to discontent among the commoners. It is more fully discussed by Perceval in his *London's Forest*. Buxton, in his book *Epping Forest*, quotes from state papers kept at the Public Record Office a royal complaint as to the behaviour of the Forest inhabitants who 'by strong hand do make havock and insufferable spoil of the woods, drive and keep the cattle upon His Majesty's said part of the land, and being disturbed by the purchaser's agents, do make pound-breaches, rescue their cattle, and beat and wound such as disturb them'. Buxton goes on to tell of sturdy opposition by his fellow countrymen of Essex who opposed a threat to the sale of Waltham Forest by the king, and who were guilty of 'fashious actions', even having the impudence to hold a 'conventicle in the very brake [bracken] where the King's stag should have been lodged for his hunting the next morning'.

When James I became king he ordered an inquiry to be made into the conditions of Waltham Forest. The neglect which this

uncovered caused him to tighten the forest laws and to revive the
severity of punishment for offences. A special forest gaol was
erected at Stratford-atte-Bow. It was conveniently situated near
the London highway so that travellers could be stopped,
searched and made to pay their dues. Tolls included fourpence
per carriage on four wheels; twopence for a conveyance without
wheels, such as a sled; fourpence for a pack of wool, and twopence for a half load. A laden horse was charged twopence, and there was a small toll on foot travellers, called
'cheminage'. These impositions and other punishments caused
one historian to write: 'I do boldly say that one man in his reign
might with more safety have killed another than a raskal deer.'
James carried his love for hunting to excess, wearing out his
courtiers and causing constant disturbance to the quiet village
inhabitants. There is a story how, one day, his favourite hound
Jewell was missing. Next day it turned up with a note tied to its
collar, 'Good Mr Jewell, we pray you speak to the King (for he
hears you every day, and so doth he not us) that it will please his
Majesty to go back to London, or else the country will be un-
done. All our provision is spent and we are not able to entertain
him longer.'

The feeling seems to have been quite antagonistic at times
towards the 'Kinge's Majesties Woode' and the 'Wild Beastes of
the Lord the King'. With their rise in numbers and a falling off
in hunting, the animals were becoming an increasing royal
nuisance. To protect his arable land the lord of the Manor of
Woodford put up enclosures, thereby incurring the displeasure
of the courts, since this was forest land. His reasonable excuse
was that he could not grow anything because of damage caused
by the deer, yet was still obliged to pay a compensation on wheat
and oats to the Crown because he was tilling forest soil.

As a result of all this disquiet, Cromwell's Long Parliament in
its first session passed an act, in 1641, to fix Waltham Forest
boundaries once more. The ensuing perambulation covered
about 60,000 acres, much of which consisted of some kind of
farmland. There was much pressure on what remained of the

woodland and heath to turn this into farmland as well. By now there were no longer any royal rights to the Forest for the king to pursue his 'pleasure, disport and recreation from the pressing cares for the publick weale and safetie, which are inseperable incident to theire kinglie office'. For the king was dead, so 'Long live the king.' But would the Forest survive?

### THE UTILITARIAN FOREST (1649–1878)

In 1653 the Long Parliament passed an act to sell off the whole of Waltham Forest for the benefit of the Commonwealth. However, Cromwell 'His Highness the Lord Protector' took matters over, and appointed a commission to see how best the Forest might be improved and disposed of. Nothing came of this, fortunately, so that it still remained intact at the Restoration in 1660; the courts and administration were able to function again, and continued to do so until the middle of the nineteenth century. This was effective in preventing any further encroachment, but in other respects the law was much to be criticised. Abuses, even flagrant violations of the forest laws, including poaching of the deer, steadily increased. At one stage it became necessary for the chief ranger of Epping Forest to order that no further red or fallow deer be killed for three years due to the severe destruction of the game during the Civil War. This took place in spite of the importation of fallow deer into the Forest by James I in 1612.

Lack of enthusiasm for hunting was particularly noticeable during the days of the Hanoverian kings. The portly bearing of their teutonic majesties, it was said, did not favour an equestrian carriage, let alone the endurance of an active chase in the saddle through brake and mire. This kind of sport was not to the liking of the eighteenth-century sovereigns, and was considered a little beneath their dignity. This lack of interest on the part of the Crown, coupled with an increasing demand for living space and farmland by a growing London—not to mention the need for timber to support the wooden navy—meant greater laxity in the forest laws. Poaching, encroachment, lawlessness and other misdemeanours became the order of the day.

The Forest straddled the main highways to the north (the old roads via Abridge and Waltham) and was ideal hunting ground of a different kind—for the footpads and highwaymen, numbering Dick Turpin among its more colourful figures. There was also a band of discharged mercenaries from the Civil War encamped near Waltham, who blackened their faces in commando fashion when out raiding. All this caused much embarrassment to the governments of the day. The Forest had outlived its usefulness; it would have to go. Meanwhile Parliament passed a Black Act for the suppression of these footpads, and nightly patrols of cavalry policed the district for the protection of travellers.

Abuses such as those perpetuated by the Lord Warden, the Hon Wellesley Pole, during his term of office in the early nineteenth century, show the extent to which the Forest had fallen into disrepute. Refusing to back up the verderers in their duty, even giving encouragement to those persons who flouted the law, the warden proceeded to sell off Forest rights which he was supposed to protect, for personal monetary gain. Forest laws were weakly administered, and the Lord Warden himself, in spite of his own wrong doing, complained to the Office of Works in 1813 of the following abuses:

a  The existence of gravel and sand pits everywhere, and material removed without restraint [the origin of many Forest ponds, see page 156].
b  Turf digging and soil and leaf-mould removal for garden use.
c  Ferns, bushes and other plants dug up for sale.
d  Bird catching and deer stealing, with greyhounds and lurchers in common use.
e  Encroachments and enclosures.
f  Timber cut and carried away at all seasons.

When officials were questioned about all this, they explained that, through lack of support from magistrates, they were repeatedly disappointed and frustrated in failing to gain convictions on trespassers and lawbreakers. The courts were inclined

*Page 35* (*above*) The famous Fairmead Oak before it was destroyed by vandals; (*below*) old method of sledge-hauling timber before the use of tractors

Page 36 (*left*) Pollarded beech trees, lopped by the commoners; (*below*) honey fungus or Forester's Curse which attacks living trees

to overlook these misdemeanours. As one keeper explained 'finding nothing done we gave up in despair'.

The last of the Forest courts took place in 1854, after having sat for nearly 700 years. A resolution had even been passed by the courts to surrender the whole question of enclosures to the lords of the Forest manors who now owned the soil, but not the forestal rights, and let them deal with any further encroachment. At one point, in 1761, a proposal was made to split the whole Forest into enclosures for planting with oak, and for fattening up lean cattle for use by the navy. The timber was to be sold to defray the cost of maintenance, or could be made into charcoal for the powder mills. Although nothing came of this move, the Office of Woods and Forests was urged in 1801 to apply to Parliament for an act to disafforest the entire area, to extinguish all rights of common and to make most of the Epping Forest acreage Crown property, as in the case of Hainault Forest across the river Roding. The prevailing idea at the time seems to have been purely utilitarian—to extract as much as possible from the Forest's soil and timber. The value of these open spaces as a lung and recreational areas for a growing London population was largely overlooked. The result, in 1851, was the full approval of the House of Commons to disafforest and totally destroy Hainault Forest. The Crown, as owners, held the manorial rights to the soil, as well as the sporting rights, and could do as they pleased. So, almost overnight, some 2,000 acres of fine old oaks, including the famous Fairlop Oak, were uprooted by steam plough and drags, and the whole operation completed in six weeks. The public at large was taken completely by surprise. Even had they realised the consequences of this act, it would have been too late to stop it.

In the case of Epping Forest, the Crown only possessed forestal rights, since the land was under ownership of the eighteen lords of the manors. What the government did here was to offer to each lord the sporting rights at £5 per acre, even forcing their hand by threats to sell to others if they refused. An inducement was that any such purchase would entitle the owner to enclose the land as private property. The manor lords can therefore hardly be blamed for erecting enclosures on their own land, which was thus freed from forestal law. It would then only be necessary to come to terms with the local commoners over their rights of lopping and grazing. Meanwhile a rise in land value, due to the increasing demand for living outside the city limits, made possible by the railway extensions, meant that there was a ready market for the sale of Forest land. As a result enclosures followed rapidly. By 1850 the Forest stood at 6,000 acres, and had diminished by half within the following twenty years, the other half becoming fenced in or built on.

It is at about this stage that farsighted and public-spirited people, worried by the increasing threat to the open spaces, began to speak up for the rights of the general public, also for the commoners themselves who were fast losing the open land on which to graze their cattle and gather firewood. A Commons Preservation Society was formed to look into this threat, and in its first task was able to save Wimbledon Common from threatened enclosure by the manor lord. Turning to Epping Forest, and with the help of some of its members who had considerable parliamentary influence, the CPS urged that an inquiry should be made. This resulted in the forming of a committee by the House of Commons, which reported in 1863 the disturbing news of a serious decline in open Forest land. It recommended that the forestal rights should be upheld on the remaining land, and that there should be no further enclosures within a 5-mile radius of London. A further inquiry two years later revealed some even more disturbing news. It was the confident attitude held by the manor lords that they were within their rights to enclose, and that nothing stood in their way except the commoners. Since in most cases such rights had already been surrendered, or compensated, the enclosure of former Forest ground was considered fully legal.

Those opposing enclosures insisted that the common rights still existed, as they always had done irrespective of ownership of the land. Such rights of common, even though rarely practised, were still sufficient excuse to resist any enclosure. Once again the parliamentary committee pressed for action, but although an act was passed to regulate the use of commonland little was done to safeguard the Forest. As a result, speculators and prospective buyers continued to assert what was believed to be legal, so that further enclosures took place.

By this time the deer were in a bad way. The last of the wild red deer had already been sent to Windsor, and the fallow had rapidly declined, as the following recorded figures show: 223 head in 1849, 86 in 1855, 48 in 1858, and only 12 (including 1 buck) in 1870. This onslaught into the Forest, the effect on its wildlife, and the gradual strangulation of the commoners' rights was now arousing much public opinion and sympathy, and no doubt many more people were made aware of the loss of these open spaces by the action of the faithful few of the CPS.

A climax was reached when the society supported the defiant act of an old Loughton villager who stood out for his ancient rights to lop the trees as his forefathers had done before him. This was the act of old Tom Willingale and his son and nephew, a story much distorted and romanticised in the telling and which has become a Forest legend. In 1865 the younger men entered the enclosed Manor of Loughton at the appointed hour to cut the branches. In consequence the lord of the manor, a much loved rector, brought an action for trespass. The court fined the younger men for damage, or seven days in gaol for default. They refused to pay, so the son Samuel, the nephew Alfred and another male relative, William Higgins, were sent to Ilford gaol. The CPS gave the commoners its aid in bringing a counter-action in support of the right to lop. The case dragged on for years and was never really decided; in the meanwhile the old man died. However, its appeal to the British people, always ready to support the underdog and see fair play, was fanned by the Press and gave public opinion more time to harden against the loss of Forest land. Even so, the manor lords felt so confident and united in their purchasing powers that they even succeeded in persuading the government to their side. The Commissioner for Works introduced a bill into Parliament, permitting the eighteen lords to retain 5,000 acres of the former Forest as part of their manors, with right to enclose, leaving a mere 600 acres open for public use, and the remaining 400 for sale at market value to compensate the commoners.

A real crisis in Forest history was now at hand. In the face of public feeling and ignoring the legal aspects of such an act, bureaucracy once more took matters into its own hands. Was Epping Forest finally to share the fate of Hainault Forest? The CPS, the only body with sufficient authority to voice public feeling, met under a cloud of despondency, debating whether to support this unhappy compromise or not. Edward North Buxton, a member of this committee, and later to become a Forest verderer, was at the meeting, and should now take up the story as related in his own book:

It is not too much to say that the fate of the Forest trembled round the table where this committee sat. If weak-kneed councils had then prevailed, the Bill would probably have been passed without opposition, and the Forest, as we know it, would have ceased to exist. Happily a spirited policy carried the day. The Bill was vigorously opposed, and dropped, and Mr Cowper-Temple subsequently carried against the Government an address to the Crown, calling upon it to preserve those parts of Epping Forest which had not been enclosed by legal authority. Public attention was now fully aroused and a new body was formed called the 'Forest Fund Society', who assisted in forcing the question to the front; but the public, without a champion, is powerless. Happily in the Corporation of the City of London a doughty one was at hand, able to contend even with the united forces of the manorial lords. It was Mr Scott, the farsighted City Chamberlain, who first suggested that the compulsory corn metage should be commuted into a small fixed duty and applied to the preservation of open spaces; and the sinews of war having been thus provided, we owe it to Mr J. T. Bedford—an able and fearless member of the Court of the Common Council—that the duty of making a supreme effort for the rescue of the Forest was vigorously pressed upon the Corporation. Owing to the happy chance that the Corporation were owners of a cemetery at Wanstead, which gave them the right of grazing a cow or two, they were able to take up the cause of the public as commoners of Epping Forest. In August 1871 a suit was commenced against the lords of the manors; which lasted more than three years, an anxious time for all concerned. The labour connected with it was enormous, owing to the multiplicity of interest involved, and obscure and intricate questions of ancient law which it raised. That it was conducted to a successful issue was largely due to the energy of the late City solicitor, Sir T. Nelson, and the zeal, combined with knowledge, of the late Sir Robert Hunter, who, an honorary solicitor to the Commons Preservation Society, had for several years made the law affecting common rights his especial study. It was contended on behalf of the lords of manors that each manor was separate, and that its commoners had no rights over the remainder of the Forest, so that in fact, if he could succeed in satisfying his own commoners, each lord of the manor could enclose or do as he liked with it. On behalf of the Corporation, on the other hand, it was urged that there never were such boundaries, and that the commoners had always enjoyed the right of 'intercommonage', as it was called—i.e. for the cattle to wander all over the Forest.

The corn metage to which Buxton refers was a mere three-quarters of a farthing tax imposed on each hundredweight of corn brought into London. From this stored-up wealth, the Corporation was able to set aside £250,000 for the eventual settlement of the forest land taken back from the manor lords and others.

The tremendous legal battle which followed lasted for three years and took the combined efforts of eighteen barristers. The final hearing lasted three days and, on 24 November 1874, Sir George Jessel, the Master of the Rolls, delivered his lucid and concise judgement. This completely endorsed the plea of the Corporation, overthrowing all enclosures, and pointing out their illegality. This was presented in such a decisive manner that its finality was never disrupted. The whole proceeding cost some £25,000. Subsequently the commissioners presented a report on the case, recommending a scheme for the future management of the Forest, and easy terms for the grantees, that is, those people who had bought land which had been illegally enclosed.

Under the pilotage of Sir H. Selwin Ibbetson, MP, later Lord Rookwood, the Act of 1878 was passed without opposition, settling the whole question of the Forest and its future. Sir Arthur Hobhouse, later Lord Hobhouse, was appointed an arbitrator to look into compensation for those manor lords, dispossessed owners, possessors of lopping rights, and so on, and also to allow a certain 'curtilage' of land around any erected buildings. Only after many years of tactful and delicate adjustments was this knotty business of compensation finally settled. The result gave the people of London a public forest of some 5,542 acres in extent.

So, on 6 May 1882, Queen Victoria was escorted by her newly appointed Ranger, the Duke of Connaught, into the Forest where a gay and spacious pavilion had been erected on the open space at High Beech. Here she met the City's Lord Mayor and the Commonalty. In a humble address in accepting the Forest for London's citizens, the Lord Mayor stated: 'as the capital of your Majesty's Empire is the largest in the World, it is fitting that its inhabitants should possess the most extensive pleasure ground'. To which the queen replied, 'It gives me the greatest satisfaction to dedicate this beautiful forest to the use and enjoyment of my people for all time.'

To mark this historic occasion, a young oak was planted. Also, out of the £7,000 compensation given to the Loughton inhabitants for the loss of their lopping rights, a building called Lopping Hall was erected along Loughton's high street. It is easily recognised by its red brick and clock-tower; over the doorway is a stone carving in relief of the loppers at work. Somewhat ironic, perhaps, was the blessing given to the Hall by the Rev John Maitland, the former lord of the manor, who originally challenged the Willingales when they entered his property.

THE AESTHETIC FOREST (1878–?)

The safeguarding and management of an area like Epping Forest depends upon the reasons for its preservation. This is clearly outlined in the Epping Forest Act of 1878, in which the following are the main points:

1 The disafforestation of Epping Forest and the termination of all Crown forestal rights.
2 The termination of the commoners' rights of lopwood.
3 The upholding of common or pasture (for cattle) and common of mast (for pigs).
4 The maintenance of the Forest in its natural aspect.
5 The granting to the public of the use of the Forest as an open and unenclosed space for recreation and enjoyment.
6 The appointment of the Corporation of the City of London as Conservators of the Forest.

The passing of this act gave the City Corporation powers to pursue a policy of honouring the wishes of Queen Victoria, the last of the sovereigns to hold forestal or hunting rights over Epping Forest. Her Majesty expressly wished that the people of London might enjoy for ever more the beauty and surroundings of her Royal Forest. As has already been noted (page 37), all rights to Forest soil were earlier owned by the eighteen lords of the manors. Today, as owners and managers, the City Corporation has full legal possession of the Forest. In a sense this means that the general public has no right on Forest soil and may only enter at the pleasure of the Corporation. This extraordinary situation is one of the legal niceties of the peculiar law relating to the use of common land, and was expressed by Sir H. Harcourt at the time of the Forest battle in this manner: 'No one has a legal right to go upon common land, but if he chooses to go on, then no one has a legal right to turn him off.'

In actual practice the public are rarely turned away, unless they happen to misbehave or infringe any of the bye-laws. All these restrictions seek to preserve the peace and security of the Forest, also its natural beauty and wildlife. In its difficult task of upholding its trust as conservators, the Corporation is to be highly commended. Lying on the doorstep of London, which continues to expand and creep round its borders, especially to the south, coupled with easy and rapid transport, the Forest is today faced with a major invasion on the part of humans. This is giving rise to many problems, not just in the Forest but in the country as a whole, and are discussed in the Epilogue.

The variety of scenery which the Forest offers, and which the conservators are seeking to maintain, is partly due to the different aspects of slope, soil conditions and degree of moisture (see Chapter 18). Also, since the Forest was made up of separate manors, the management of each was different. This has given individual character to each part.

A few of the more outstanding features can be noted briefly. Starting in the north, beyond Epping Town, lies the separate portion of about 270 acres, the Lower Forest, known for centuries past as Old Wyntre Wood. It is a somewhat dense woodland of mixed oak and hornbeam with a few ash, on a heavy soil of boulder clay, often waterlogged in winter. It supports a rich undergrowth of thorn, briar and holly. Botanically it is one of the best areas in the whole Forest, and contains many flowers, liverworts, mosses and ferns. This may be partly due to its dampness, its remoteness, and its difficult penetration, so that people usually keep to the rides. One of these, the Old Stump Road, was once part of the old road between London and Harlow. It connects at one end with the main road to Harlow, and at the other with the road into Coopersale.

Moving south of Epping, there is a drier soil with better drainage in Epping Thicks. A heavy concentration of holly makes ideal cover for the fallow deer, and this is one of the few places where these shy animals may be seen. The Green Ride running through it passes the British camp at Ambersbury Banks, close to which are some fine unpollarded beeches and hornbeams. This pleasant ride continues alongside Long Running, an open grassy plain just north of the road intersection at the Wake Arms Inn. It is attractively covered with patches of bracken and heather, and small grooves of silver birch. Frequent forest fires have kept Long Running more or less open, and have provided the author with opportunities for some interesting ecological studies in colonisation (see page 176).

This grassy place is the home of the adder and common lizard, and was formerly a breeding ground for the nightjar. Silver birches increase in numbers and are concentrated along the north side of the road to Theydon Bois. Crossing this to the south we enter Theydon Highwood, consisting mainly of beeches which were regularly pollarded in the past. A thinning policy carried out by the conservators has made room for a number of sturdy young spear trees which are filling in the spaces. This area is pleasantly broken by a number of small clearings containing thorn and bracken, also some old crab trees. Under the beeches lies a rich carpet of leaves, providing a home for a large variety of fungi which appear in autumn. It is one of the favourite collecting areas for the mycologist (see page 144).

This is the Theydon manor in which is situated the Buxton estate of Birch Hall, now partly given over to a deer sanctuary. Adjoining this is the Loughton manor, largely comprising pollarded trees. It extends across the Loughton road southwards to the outskirts of the town at Staples Hill, the venue of the old loppers (see page 77). In the centre of this manor lies Monk Wood. This is the very heart of the Forest, and here can be seen some of the finest beeches by following the Green Ride to Bellringers Hollow, then branching off into Little Monk Wood. The trees are untouched by the axe, and stand on a beautiful hill whose floor at the right season is carpeted with thick green clumps of cushion-moss. This historic piece of forest land is discussed in the *Essex Naturalist*, which gives an explanation as to its origin (see Bibliography). In it there are some ponds close to Loughton, at Goldings Hill and below Baldwin's Hill. These contain some interesting pondlife, both plant and animal. One of the prettiest of the Forest ponds is the Blackweir Hill pond right inside Monk Wood—the 'Lost Pond' so-named by Mr James Brimble in his excellent pictorial book on the Forest. The second British encampment is close by.

On the far side of the New Epping Road, built in 1840, lie the two woods known as St Thomas's and Honey Lane Quarters. These cover the western side of the Forest, on a slope overlooking the Lea Valley. Careful thinning of old timber has opened up some fine views, including glimpses of the famous abbey at Waltham. On quiet days this is a good area to visit in the hope of glimpsing the deer. They tend to gather in the woods around Woodredon Farm and inside the grounds of Copt Hall estate. South of the Wake Arms, also on the western slopes of the Forest, lies High Beech. This is almost the highest point in the area and commands a fine view on clear days across the home counties. In this neighbourhood, especially all around the little church nearby, is a charming wood of birches. Their graceful form is in strong contrast to the sturdy beeches of Hill Wood which rival those in Monk Wood. Descending the hill through this wood, we reach the open space of Fairmead, once the traditional meeting places of the Easter Chase (see page 68). The old Fairmead Oak, which used to stand there and must have witnessed many a gathering, is no more. Dead for many years, it was set on fire and destroyed by vandals in the late 1940s. The attraction of Fairmead lies in its thorn bushes, both whitethorn and blackthorn, also bramble and briar. This is the spot to visit on a mild May or June evening in order to hear the nightingale.

Farther south, as far as Chingford, lies a dense and heavily pollarded area mainly of oak and hornbeam. This includes Hawk Wood and Bury Wood, part of the Chingford manor. Extensive thinning since the Corporation took over has encouraged a number of spear trees to grow up. Buxton refers to the removal of some 300 spindly oaks during one year. The ultimate aim in all this thinning, which still goes on, is to achieve quality in the trees, rather than quantity, so that more will grow to the fine proportion of the Grimston Oak, named after the cricketer. The tree is in a clearing where a number of rides intersect just north of the Connaught Water. This stretch of water, the largest in the Forest, was named after the Duke of Connaught, the first Ranger appointed by Queen Victoria. Between it and Chingford is the open expanse of Chingford Plain, used as a golf-course, and the meeting place of one of the bank holiday fairs. At a high spot along the Ranger's Road stands the old building called the Queen Elizabeth's Hunting Lodge, now used as a museum. Somewhat isolated from the main Forest is Lord's Bushes, a wood of some 100 acres adjoining Knighton Wood, the former property of the Buxton family. The first contains some fine oaks and beeches, and the latter an attractive lake.

South of Chingford, in the Walthamstow manor, there are plenty of small hornbeams and oaks but few beeches. The area is somewhat patchy, due to some encroachment in the past and also to the activities of the gravel diggers. Numbers of these workings have since filled up as ponds, especially towards the southern end of the Forest on the open grasslands of Leytonstone and Wanstead Flats. Finally, there is Wanstead Park, now part of the Forest, and at one time part of the great eighteenth-century estate of Wanstead House. The trees are mainly elm, with a few oak and beech, and a number of sycamore.

This, briefly, is the Epping Forest of today, visited by thousands of Londoners, who go there for a variety of reasons. The majority seem content to make for one of the open spaces close to the roadways or inns, to enjoy a picnic or merely to sit in the open air. There are recreational facilities, such as the established golf links and cricket pitches, mostly unenclosed so that public access is not restricted, unless a game is in progress. Fishing is permitted on most ponds, and there are opportunities for boating. On bank holidays the fairs on Chingford Plain and Wanstead Flats attract numbers of people who enjoy this kind of thing.

In contrast, there are those who prefer the quieter pleasures of rambling or natural history pursuits, painting or simply quiet meditation in some lonely spot. It is still possible on a weekday to wander through deeper parts without meeting anyone. In particular, the Forest has become famous for its natural history, and many London and neighbouring clubs and societies make it a regular rendezvous. There are also field centres, for children as well as adults, which organise outings and residential courses. Full advantage is now taken of all that this famous Forest can offer to the London-weary resident, yet wherever he goes the incessant throb of the great metropolis is never out of hearing, day or night. It serves as a constant reminder of the wisdom of those who saw in this ancient but precious open space a quiet retreat for recreation and refreshment, more so perhaps for the brain than the body. Buxton saw it in this way:

> It is in its varied aspects that the greatest refreshment is to be found for the eye and the brain, weary of dead walls and the turmoil of streets. The general opinion, so unmistakably evinced, that the Forest shall remain forest and not be civilised into a park, is but the expression of a true instinct. May the people of London for all time continue to draw full draughts at this source, and to profit by the companionship and teaching of nature.

## 2

# THE LAWES FORREST

If any freeman shall chase away a Dere, or a wilde beast out of the Forest, whether the same be done by chaunce, or of a set purpose, so that thereby the wild beaste is forced by swift running to lyll out the tong, or to breathe with his tong out of his mouth, he shall paie to the King ten shillings amends for the same offence; but if he be a seruile person, then he shall double the same recompence; but if he be a bondman, then shall he lose his skinne.

Carta de Foresta (1217)

Laws are made to be changed or broken, a wise counsellor once said. One might also add that the making of a law is an admission of failure, in that it betrays a lack of agreement or understanding of another's point of view.

With the early villagers and their way of life, which was to share the land for common use, the right to do so was a law unto itself. The land use was their birthright, to live on and use as they pleased, as they had always done. However, when the overlords came along to impose their own rights, or rather pleasures, to hunt on the very same land, laws became necessary if only to protect the very things they wished to destroy, namely the game. It is perhaps a sad reflection on any blood-sport that, in order to kill, one must also preserve and protect, in order to perpetuate the pastime; hence the modern gaming laws and close seasons in existence today.

In doing this, and thereby protecting the wild animals by laws, the Danes, and in particular the Normans, were among the pioneers of the conservation movement we hear so much about today. It is now realised that in a world so disturbed by man, where the natural balance can so easily be upset, a species of animal may soon die out. It could also increase alarmingly, and some sort of scientific control is necessary, that is, conservation. To maintain a steady flow of deer and other game animals, the medieval huntsmen took over much of the common or wasteland which was already used by the farmers for their cattle grazing, pig feeding and wood gathering. In effect they created open game parks. On these the farming activities were allowed by the Crown, for reasons explained elsewhere (see page 24).

At the same time what were called the commoners' rights were strictly controlled by means of forest laws which gave protection to the deer. Offences within the Kinge's Forrest against the vert and venison (the trees and deer), were dealt with in stages through the various forest courts. The punishment and its degree of severity was made to fit the crime. The example taken from the Forest Charter, which heads this chapter, might suggest a kind of ruthlessness and severity, which could only be condoned by a barbaric ruler and which must have struck terror in the hearts of the commoners. It often meant the life of a serf for that of a royal beast. This was precisely its intention, to make a quick retribution by means of a cruel punishment after the merest trial. The sight of a mutilated brother or father would have acted as a constant and salutary warning to others not to trifle with the law. Such severity may have been the rule in the reign of the first Norman dictators. Later on, the Forest law became more lenient, but at the same time much more cumbersome. It was suited to harass the offenders rather than hurt. Months, even years, might go by before punishment was finally passed.

The Select Pleas mention three forest courts. Minor or first offenders were handled by the Court of Attachment, sometimes called the Forty-day Court. It sat every sixth week, and was attended by the verderers and foresters. It was held in each forest, or in one of its divisions or bailiwicks, mainly to hear cases of trespass against the 'vert' (timber). It was originally called the Woodmote. Trespass of a more serious nature, as against 'venison' (deer and other game) was tried at the Justice Seat, that is, the High Court of the Lord Justice in Eyre (see Glossary). Such cases were usually tried by jury and took the form of an inquiry or inquisition.

The deer carcass was disposed of in the following manner:

> If any beast of forest were found dead or wounded, an inquisition was to be held by four neighbouring townships of the Forest. The finder of the deer was to be put before the Justice at Eyre at their next pleas; the flesh to be sent to a neighbouring spittal house [place for consumptives] or given to the sick and poor; the head and skin to be given to the freeman of the neighbouring township; and the arrow to be presented to the verderer. The offender, if caught, was 'attached' to appear before the Justice Seat.

With deer stealing, always a serious offence, the punishment varied with the situation at the time of arrest. A man could be arrested at 'Stablestand', that is, found in a compromising situation; today we would call it loitering with intent. Or he could be at 'Dog's Draw', and apprehended in the possession of dogs in suspicious circumstances. 'Bloody Hand' meant being caught with blood on one's person, or revealing some other clue to suggest that a deer had been poached. The most serious situation was 'Bare Back', actually being caught with a poached deer or, as we say, with the goods. This was the crime for which a culprit was once mutilated or banished. At a later period, he went straight to gaol and could only be freed by a writ from the king, or the Justice of the Forest who was his appointed deputy. If arrested or convicted of taking venison, there was a heavy ransom, or imprisonment for a year and a day. The prisoner was released only if he could find a pledge. Otherwise he might have had to abjure the realm. Normally a defendant was bound over and released on bail, or by a writ from twelve persons who undertook to produce him at the next Eyre. Sometimes a whole village might have to face the court for not having produced a culprit. The village was then 'in mercy' to the Justice Seat, and liable to an 'amercement' or fine.

Inquisitions of this kind gradually fell into disuse, and were later superseded by a more general kind of inquiry, called a Swainmote. Manwood, in his *Lawes Forrest*, mentions such a court, the Swainamota, as being held three times a year to try offences adjourned from the Court of Attachment. Whether or not such did exist in the early years of forest law, the Swainmote eventually came into general use for dealing broadly with all forest offences. The possibilities are that it is an ancient court, as the name derives from the Anglo-Saxon *swangemot*, a meeting place for the swineherds. It was an open court presided over by the keepers of the royal forests, in accordance with the Carta de Foresta of 1217. Its purpose was to arrange for the depasturing of pigs in the acorn season, the clearance of cattle from the forest during the deer's fawning season, and so on. At this court, attended by the verderers and a jury of forest freeholders, the steward would record the proceedings, endorse licences, swear in officers, and charge the guilty to appear at the next Justice Seat.

These cases were stored up each year, then presented before the Justice of the Forest. This worthy moved around, holding his Eyres in the various towns much after the fashion of the itinerant circuit judges who used to visit the different county towns in the days of America's 'Wild West'. A ceremony enacted at the Justice Seat shows the power this court held over its officials, quite apart from the offenders. The chief forester and the chief woodward, kneeling, would each present to the Marshall of the Court the symbol of his office: the woodward an axe and the forester his horn. These were retained by the court during its session. Justice Seats for Waltham Forest were held at convenient spots along the King's Highway between London and Colchester, and included Stratford-atte-Bow, Ilford and Chelmsford. The Swainmote would meet at suitable centres in the Forest, such as Chigwell, Buckhurst Hill and Brentwood. The Court of Attachment was for many years held at Chigwell in the King's Head, later made famous by Dickens in his *Barnaby Rudge*.

Foresters, verderers and twelve jurors attended these courts. In the Select Pleas we read:

> First we will and ordain for us and our heirs that with respect to all trespasses hereafter committed in our forests, against our vert and venison, the foresters, within whose bailiwicks such trespass may chance to be committed, do present the same at the next Swainmote before the foresters, verderers and all other ministers aforesaid, by the oath as well of the knights as of other good men, and loyal men of the neighbouring parts where the trespass so presented shall be committed, let the truth be fully inquired; and when the truth has been so inquired, let those presentiments be solemnly confirmed by the common accord and consent of all the ministers aforesaid, and let them be sealed with their seals. And if any indictment be made in any other way, let it be held entirely void.

The sheer legal verbosity of the above will suggest that even in those days of law enforcement, the legal brains were careful to avoid any loopholes which might come up during such an inquisition. Frequently such a plea was headed by a long preamble stressing the rights and wisdom of the sovereign in whose name they were enacted.

At one time the trespass against vert or venison was treated as a crime and punished accordingly. As the law mellowed, however, one gains the impression that the trespasses were being treated more in the light of encroachment which could then be compounded on payment of a so-called rent rather than a fine. Indeed, the Crown was sometimes lenient enough to allow a trespasser of land to retain what he had squatted on, provided that he paid his dues. It all helped to swell the royal coffers. Over this question of the fines which were imposed for any illegal enclosures, the lists for these in the court rolls read more like an account sheet. Once the trespass was paid, then the new owner could go on using the land at an annual rental. This worked out at a shilling an acre per crop of winter corn, and sixpence an acre of spring corn. Thus the illegal enclosure could be amerced by the original fine, after which a yearly payment of rent, rather than a penalty, became due.

D

Heavy ransoms became rare, but these fines were applied to laymen and officials alike, whoever broke the law by enclosing illegally. Some charity was shown by pardoning the poor and by taking into consideration the time spent in gaol. The following list of fines for trespass is quoted by Fisher, and was recorded at the Eyre in Surrey, held in 1272, for trespass in Guildford Park:

| | | | |
|---|---|---|---|
| Thomas de Bois | o. | 13. | 4 |
| Ralph de Slyfuld | o. | 6. | 8 |
| Alan de Slyfuld | o. | 6. | 8 |
| John atte Hook | o. | 6. | 8 |
| Robert le King | o. | 6. | 8 |
| Peter Long | o. | 6. | 8 |
| John de Aldham | 13. | 6. | 8 |
| Andrew de Fremelesworth | o. | 10. | o |
| Geoffrey de Brayhoof | 2. | 13. | 4 |
| John son of Aubrey | o. | 6. | 8 |
| Peter Dodleston | pardoned | | |

One very important person of the courts, called variously the forest warden, steward or custodian, carried a rank and authority resembling that of a county sheriff. Fines imposed on offenders against vert, but not against venison, were the recognised perquisites of the warden, and could work out over the year as a handsome income. The warden also claimed all browst, or deer-browsing wood, and could claim any commoner's beast found straying or unclaimed on the forest land. Buyers and sellers of timber paid him compensation. All this was done legally and has nothing to do with the abuses quoted by Fisher on page 34.

The Norman kings were not particularly enamoured of the Church, even though they allowed them certain favours. For instance, in the two most favoured forests of Waltham and Windsor, a number of fee deer were set aside for the 'entertainment of foreign princes and their agents and ambassadors, also to the Bishop of Waltham and the Abbess of Barking, because the nearness of these two Forests unto the City doth give much pleasure to both'. At the same time the clerics were placed on a similar footing to others when it came to offences on forest soil.

The bishop of the district was instructed by the Justice in Eyre to cause the appearance of any cleric accused of trespass at the court. This caused a lot of wrangling between the ecclesiastics and forest officials, and little love was lost between Church and Crown. It is for this reason that historians treat with some caution the early historic records, since these were mostly kept by the clerks of the day (the clerics or churchmen).

There is reason to think that, out of spite, they grossly exaggerated the exploits of the Conqueror. For instance, there is the mention of landgrabbing and destruction of vills by the king, in order to extend his forest domain. William Cobbett, the author of *Rural Rides*, ridicules the idea that whole towns and vills were razed by the dictator. There was no need for this since there was still plenty of room for man and beast. Also, most of the forest soil was unsuited to farming, being either heavily wooded or unfertile, and so thinly populated. This is precisely the situation with many of our open commons and heaths today. They still remain as waste on poor, gravel or sandy soils.

At one time the importance of venison over vert was reflected in the degree of punishment. Stealing a deer was far more serious than felling a tree or illegally encroaching on forest land. Later on the position became reversed, so that the timber and land became more important than the deer. In the New Forest the need for trees and grazing land actually led up to a Deer Removal Act in 1851. It was passed more as an act of grace by the Crown under pressure from the commoners. The removal of deer would mean more pasture for cattle. In return the Crown asked for some 16,000 acres of forest soil on which to grow timber so as to benefit the country.

Dr Thomas Fuller, a great churchman in Charles II's reign and curate of Waltham Abbey (1649–58), writes: 'Fourteen years since one might have seen whole herds of red and fallow deer. But these late licentious years have been such a Nimrod that all at this present are destroyed, though I could wish this were the worst effect which our woeful wars have produced.' The Commonwealth brought a halt to all the splendour of the royal sport, and it even became necessary to restock the Forest at the Restoration. By then the heart had gone from the ancient pastime and the land was considered more a place for growing timber. Samuel Pepys certainly took full advantage of his position as adviser to the Admiralty. Many a forest oak ended its life by way of Barking Creek, and so to the naval dockyards at Deptford and Woolwich. In this manner forest timber continued to supply the navy until the 1720s, by which date most of the best had been felled. The poor quality of many of today's oaks in the Forest, largely a collection of miserable and dying pollards, is a silent reproach to this robbery and total disregard for the future. However, some healthy young oaks are now becoming established in parts of the Forest.

# 3

# THE KINGE'S DERE

Div's greedye persones having in their hands sundry closes and pastures within our said Forest have for the pryvate gayne and proffett so enclosed the seid closes and pastures withe such unreasonable hedges and dyches, as our said Deare have been utterlye defraudyd contrarye to our Lawes, and to the great famyshinge and destruction of our said Deare.
a royal complaint in the reign of Edward VI (1548)

'A park without deer', said Richard Jeffries, 'is like a wall without pictures.' Deer have lived in Britain's parks and estates for centuries, but they have also roamed the woodlands since pre historic times. Today there are probably as many as ever in some of the woods and mountain areas, including a number which have been introduced. Only two species are considered to be truly native; their remains are known in association with Palaeolithic man going back many thousands of years. These are the red deer, the largest wild animal in Britain today, and the tiny roe deer. These two species, especially the former, were hunted by our ancestors, who cooked the meat over their fires, carved weapons and tools from the bones and antlers, and left paintings of them on the walls of their caves.

Both red and roe deer once lived in Epping Forest. After hunting ceased, the remainder of the red deer were rounded up in the 1820s and sent to Windsor Park. The tiny roe, long extinct in the Forest, was introduced by Edward North Buxton as an experiment to re-establish it. In February 1884, two buck and four does, caught from a wood in Dorset, were brought up by

van and set free in the Forest. For some years they continued to
survive, even producing some kids, but finally disappeared.
This commendable but unsuccessful move may have failed
because of disturbance or unsuitable terrain. Roe seem to prefer
heavy underwood, especially among young conifer, and in Britain
are usually to be found among the forestry plantations. Very few
conifers occur in Epping Forest. Also, roe keep together in small
family parties, rather than in herds, and tend to remain in one
area. A gradual increase in visitors since the act was passed may
have caused them to disperse into quieter places away to the
north.

Today only fallow deer are to be found, and these very few in
number. Here again, the constant disturbance may be the cause
of their decline, apart from the hazards of traffic and molesting
by dogs. Ease of travel, increase in the number of cars and
greater activity in outdoor pastimes, such as rambling, horse-
riding and natural history, have all combined to disturb the
former privacy of the Forest. Signs of human footprints and
horse tracks along the rides show that no corner remains untouched. The presence of deer has always been essential for the
purpose for which a royal forest was created—as a place for
hunting. In this respect, however, hunting of the deer as a royal
sport was carefully distinguished from other forms of venerie.
Manwood, in his *Treatise and Discourse of the Lawes of the
Forrest* in 1744, described a forest as: 'certain Territories of
woody grounds and fruitful pastures, priuileged for wild beasts
and foules of Forest, Chase and Warren, to rest and abide in, in
the safe protection of the Kinge, for his princely delight and
pleasure'. Manwood made careful distinction between the three
classes of hunting territories: 'in these three things a Forrest
doth differ from a Chase, that is to say, in its particular Lawes, in
its particular officers, and in certain courts . . . A Chase may be
in the hand of a subject, which a Forrest in its proper nature
cannot be' (see Glossary). A carefully observed code of hunting
can be seen in this, even to the ranking of the beasts themselves.

The following is a list from Manwood, based on an earlier

treatise formed by Tovi, the standard-bearer to King Canute. The Royal Beastes of Forrest included the hart and hind (male and female red deer), the wolf, wild boar and hare, and were hunted exclusively by the sovereign, or by royal favour. Beastes of Chase or Park were the buck and doe (male and female fallow deer), and roe deer, marten and fox. These were usually hunted by the barons, and the noblemen and ladies of the court, also by visiting dignitaries and the Church. Actually, the law did not normally recognise these distinctions, and trespass against red and fallow deer were treated in court with the same penalties. It also appears that the hare and wolf were given no special protection in law. In any case the wolf was exterminated fairly early in history. The hare has a more interesting record. In some forests it was listed, but in others considered a 'nusance' because it was to 'the general disquieting of the Kinge's dere'. Its importance as a beast of warren came later with the partridge and pheasant, and today all three are treated as game. The rabbit, or coney as it was then called, was also a beast of warren but has never received the protection of the game laws, even today. It is, in fact, still treated as vermin, whereas at one time it was preserved in so-called warrens as a valuable food and fur animal, especially by the Normans who introduced it to Britain.

A more general division of the forest animals placed them under two broad headings. The larger beasts, such as the deer, bear and boar, were named the animals of 'swete fewte' (sweet foot), and the smaller ones, such as fox, cat and marten, as those of 'stynkinge fewte'.

For Waltham Forest, the fox and marten were given the lowly rank of 'vermyn' and 'raskalls', and the wolf is not even mentioned, even though special wolf-dogs (*Canis lupararus*) are spoken of in the time of Edward III. The wild boar appears in the records up to the twelfth century. Wild cattle are mentioned in Caesar's time, but were never considered beasts of forest. They may well have died out before organised hunting began, or perhaps were domesticated by then. The name of the wildcat often appears in the records, but this could be a confusion with the marten 'cat', an entirely different animal once hunted for its fur. During the fourteenth century the roe was 'demoted' to the rank of beast of warren as it was thought to disturb, even drive away, the more noble fallow deer.

Of equal importance in hunting circles has been the ancient pastime of hawking, or falconry. This goes back into antiquity, even more so, perhaps, than deer hunting. It is recorded from ancient China, and was undoubtedly followed by the Romans in Britain, and certainly by the Normans. The first English sporting treatise on the subject, *The Book of St Albans*, was penned by the scholarly Lady Juliana Berners, prioress of Sopewell Nunnery near St Albans in 1486; it is one of the earliest English printed works. The book was obviously directed at the nobility, the sport being above lesser mortals. In falconry the same kind of social ranking order is evident in the use of birds of prey, for the pursuit of game, as in the following old rhyme:

> To the emperor the eagle
> To the king the gyr-falcon [*Falco islandicus*]
> To the prince the falcon gentle [*F. palumbarius*]
> To the earl the peregrine [*F. perigrinus*]
> To the lady the merlin
> To the young squire the hobby
> To the yeoman the goshawk
> To the priest the sparrow-hawk
> And to the servant the kestrel.

That the royal beasts were considered the most favoured of the forest dwellers, even more so than the human residents, may be judged from the many restrictions placed upon the latter. Apart from the strict enforcement of the law, and the severe and cruel punishments meted out for poaching, there were many other do's and don'ts for people to bear in mind. No form of hunting was permitted after dark, and no disguise such as a hood or mask was allowed to cover the face. The possession of a crossbow or nets without permission was also an offence, even with keepers. Only a 'priuileged' few might retain arms or dogs. The siting of alehouses and the planting of nut trees was controlled, so as to prevent gathering of people which might alarm the deer. All holdings of private land on forest soil which were enclosed had to have fences or hedges no higher than a deer could jump, thereby allowing the animals free passage wherever they happened to go. This annoyance, especially if crops were damaged, was somewhat eased by a subtle form of poaching which went on. Deer were trapped on enclosed land by the construction of deer-leaps, or salteries. These were ramps leading up to a gap in a hedge over which a deer could leap inwards but was prevented by a deep inner ditch from jumping out. During the disturbing days after the Civil War, numerous Forest dwellings were occupied by deer stealers, and many a haunch of venison found its way into a cellar or some hidden recess beneath the floor. The deer meat was eaten or sold as 'black sausage' or 'black mutton', and could even be purchased openly in the butcher's shops of the Forest towns until the turn of this century.

Dogs in unauthorised possession within the forest area were hock-sinewed, that is, hamstrung so as to prevent them from chasing the deer. To become exempt from this cruel practice, a dog could be lawed (recognised in law). In Canute's time dogs could not be kept by anyone lower than a thane. This mutilation, called *genuiscissio*, only applied to the early years of hunting. Later on, the three inner claws of each fore-foot were expeditated (cut off). Manwood in his *Lawes Forrest* gives a careful description of this operation: 'The mastive being brought to set one of his fore-feet upon a piece of wood eight inches thicke and a foot square, the one with a mallet setting a chissell two inches broad upon the three claws of his fore-foot, at one blowe doth smite them clean off.' The performance was, at least, painless to the dog. In general, only certain breeds were expeditated, such as mastiffs which were probably of main use as guard dogs. The two recognised kinds of hunting dogs were the running hounds, or *leporarios*, of the deerhound or greyhound build, and the scenting hounds, or *braschetos*, which were more of the harrier or bracket type. Dogs which would not seriously disturb the deer were exempt from mutilation, so long as they were small enough to pass through the great stirrup of King Rufus; this would have meant any dog up to about fox-terrier size. A facsimile of one such large stirrup of the old hunting days is preserved in the Queen's Hall at Lyndhurst in the New Forest. Certain place-names, such as the Isle of Dogs at the mouth of the Lea, and Houndsditch in the East End, have probably originated from the kennels of hounds kept there and used for hunting. Wildfowling, too, for which retriever dogs were used, must have gone on throughout the Essex marshes, where there are now buildings and dockland.

Hunting the deer was a royal prerogative, but from time to time the forest officials, the knights templars, foreign dignitaries and such ecclesiastics as the Abbot of Waltham and the Abbess of Barking, were permitted to hunt. For this a special royal warrant was granted, and a warrantable stag or buck would be selected by the keepers who kept an eye on the herds. Also, from time to time, again by royal favour, deer were selected as gifts of venison for various people. These were called fee deer. The favour was withdrawn at times when the number of deer fell below a certain level. Every time a deer was killed during a hunt, or even found dead from wounds, the keeper in whose beat it was found was instructed to sound the 'morte' (death) by blowing on his horn. This warned the neighbourhood of the event. The following record of such an incident, quoted by Fisher, appeared at the Essex Swainmote at Buckhurst Hill in 1495: 'The kepe fande a sowyr dede in Chyngeforde hawe, the iiij day of Auguste, and the kepe bleu for the woodwards, and no mane woed anseure.' Presumably there had been some dirty work afoot! 'Sowyr' probably stands for the modern fourth-year fallow buck called a sore.

The hunting season, or grease time (French: *graisse*) varied from one animal to the next. One edict gave the following:

Hart and buck (male, red and fallow)  from the Feast of St
  John the Baptist (6 July) to Holyrood Day (25 September).
Hind and doe (female, red and fallow)  from Holyrood to
  Candlemas (14 February).

Fox   from Christmas to Ladyday.
Hare  from Michaelmas to Midsummer-day.
Boar  from Christmas to Candlemas.

Any conservationist will agree that, if a species is to survive and flourish, then the habitat to which it is adapted is as important, if not more so, than the species itself. With deer in Britain it is the wooded countryside which is best to their liking and, provided they can freely roam undisturbed among the bushes and trees, they will do so. The Norman huntsman was well aware of this, and so took a firm control on the land by making the laws to protect his animals, also by prohibiting any illegal enclosure which would hinder them. Even so, this practice went on, and from time to time was deplored by the sovereign, as in the case of the complaint of Edward VI which heads this chapter. In those days hunting was paramount on forest land. Later on, as this interest waned, more and more land was taken over and enclosed, partly to increase the Crown's revenue by means of taxes and rentals, and also to make way for farmland and housing. Ironically, this went contrary to the very purpose for which a forest was created, to the 'great famyshinge and destruction of our said Deare'. For nearly 600 years the sovereigns and their retinues hunted the woods of Waltham Forest with horse and hound, longbow and crossbow, and made merry at the abbey centres of Barking and Waltham. To quote one old rhyme:

> The second Charles of England
> Rode forth one Christmastide
> to hunt a gallant stag of ten
> of Chingford woods the pride.

The esteem with which the Royal Forest of Waltham was regarded by the Crown is expressed in the Exchequer Bills of Charles I:

> alwaies and especiallie and above all theire other fforests prized and estimated by the Kinges Majestie and his said noble progenitors the Kinges and Queenes of this Realme of England, and well for his and theire own pleasure, disport and recreation from those pressing cares for the publique weale and safetie which are

inseperable incident to their Kinglie office, as for the entertainment of foreyne Princes and Embassadors, thereby to show unto them the magnificense of the Kinges and Queenes of this Realme.

Henry VIII was a great lover of venerie, and spent many a day in the Forest at his park at Fayremeade. This covered a large area between High Beech and Chingford, and included the 'Great Stonedings' now known as the Queen Elizabeth's Hunting Lodge. This district was later to become the meeting place of the annual Epping Hunt at Easter. Meanwhile the royal monarchs made merry:

> The hunt is up, the hunt is up,
> And it is well-nigh day
> And Harry our King is gone hunting
> To bring the deer to bay.

From Duke William to Charles II, the emphasis in the use of forests was as a roya lpleasure ground for hunting. Those who hunted by royal favour did so 'at their peryle accordyng as the Kinge's lawes wyle suffer them'. Kings and nobles usually hunted the stags, and a full-grown twelve-pointer, called a 'royal', was of sufficiently noble build to become the king's personal quarry. An 'imperial', with more than twelve points, was even better. Where such an animal eluded the royal chase it was given its freedom, and then became a Royal Hart Proclaimed. The ladies and noblemen, especially the women, usually preferred the gentler chase of the fallow doe during the summer season. The deer was pursued to horse with hounds and crossbow.

With this weapon, we are told, good Queen Bess could hit a deer, as it bounded past her ambush, 'with great surety'. The skill required to do this, probably at close range, is not so remarkable, especially if one stood on the steps of a hunting lodge and took aim as the keepers drove the frightened animal past. The queen and her buckhounds made numerous visits to her hunting lodge at Lyndhurst in the New Forest, and possibly, too, she used the building named after her at Chingford. The ladies' sport lasted from 24 June to 14 September. Anne Boleyn and her daughter Elizabeth are the only English queens who stand out prominently as Dianas of the chase. The neglect into which the Forest had fallen since the days of Henry VIII was excused by James I, who said that 'by reason of their sexe' Queen Mary and Queen Elizabeth had failed to do justice to that 'most royall and princelike pleasure'. Quite probably the queens and consorts, as well as their ladies at court, preferred the gentler sport of hawking. Hunting the noble stag or no, the gentler sex must have admired its splendid bearing, for it is said, among those who have studied the baffling changes and creations of womanly fashion, that the high and elaborate head-dresses of certain periods were inspired by the spread of the stag's antlers, a crowning adornment worth imitating.

During winter the men hunted the buck from 1 November to 2 February. Every assistance at each meet was given by the keepers who knew the area and the movements of the deer. Reports of every hunt were recorded in the Rolls at the Swainmote. In certain cases the freemen were entitled the privilege to hunt the fee deer which could be 'most convenyently sparyd by the outsyght and discrecion of the lieutenant or ranger of the area'. Even the commoners were allowed to take part on official occasions, so as to promote 'frendschyppe and amytie' between forest officials and forest residents, that is, the commoners.

Since earliest times, the Church has enjoyed many hunting privileges, as well as ownership of forest soil. The bishops of London, such as Erkenwald, fourth Bishop of St Paul's, probably joined in many a hunt with the seven Saxon monarchs (see page 29). That the Church had a say in forest affairs is hinted at in the oft-quoted rhyming charter of Edward the Confessor, which lies in the British Museum. In it the Bishop Wolston, together with one Sweyn of Essex, act as witness to the appointment of Randolph Peperking to the office of Keeper of the Forest:

> Ich Edward Koning
> Have yeven of my forest the keping
> Of the hundred of Chelmer and Dancing

To Randolph Peperking and his kindling [heirs]
. . . and therefore Iche macce him my booke;
Witness the Bishop of Wolston
. . . and Sweyne of Essex, our Brother.

Shortly we shall read of the civic hunting in the Forest of Waltham and the ludicrous sight of portly City dignitaries in their unaccustomed seats. Equally comic must have been the spectacle of the jovial, fat friars on their hunting forays, riding, Perceval quotes, on equally 'fatte hors and joly and gaye sadeles and bridilis ryngynge be the weye'.

Some sovereigns lavished gifts and attention on the Church. Others, such as Henry VIII, despised this, and the Dissolution must have sadly restricted the sporting activities of the monastic centres. On the other hand, Henry III recognised the position of the Abbess of Barking as ranking a baroness. According to feudal custom, the Abbess was obliged to supply her quota of men during times of war. Being a woman, she herself was excused, but could nevertheless enjoy the privileges of her position. The king ordered the chief forester to:

> allow the Abbess of Barking her reasonable estovers [kindling wood] in her wood at Hainault for her firing, her cooking and her brewing, if she has been accustomed so to do in the time of our Lord King John our father; also to permit the said Abbess to have her dogs to chase hares and foxes within the bailiwick if she was accustomed to have them in the time of our aforesaid father.

A curious church ceremony formerly held in London is very suggestive of some ancient pagan mythology handed down from ages past. This took place as part of an annual service at St Paul's on 25 January, the Feast of the Conversion of St Paul, and at the Commemoration, on 29 June. At the earlier feast, a doe— and, at the latter, a buck—was delivered at the cathedral steps and received before the altar by the dean and chapter dressed in 'copes and proper vestments, with garlands of roses on their heads'. The deer's head was separated, and the carcass sent to the kitchens. The antlered head was then fixed to a staff and carried

66

before the cross in procession round the church, until met by the
keeper at the west door. He then sounded the 'morte', or 'death'
call, and this was picked up by others all around the City.
Camden suggests that this was a pagan custom incorporated into
the Christian church—possibly a ceremony practised by the
Romans in the Temple of Diana when it occupied the site of St
Paul's. Deer ceremonies are not unknown today; one of these
takes place annually at Abbots Bromley in Staffordshire. This
serves to remind us of the close and ancient ties which have
existed between man the hunter and his quarry the deer, as
mentioned at the beginning of this book.

There is another side to this hunting of the Epping Forest
deer. Apart from the royal hunts, there have been, since very
early times, certain favours and concessions granted by the king
to his people, enabling them also to enjoy the pleasure of the
hunt. One must bear in mind that hunting, since early Palaeolithic days, is something in the blood of man, whether king or
commoner, and is a natural outlet for his enthusiasm and surplus
physical energy. Today we tend to curb this desire, or to divert
it into some harmless, civilised, but no less energetic channel,
such as football or field photography.

Of all the civic hunts which went on perhaps the best known
is the Easter Chase of Essex. The Eastertide holiday provided an
opportunity for people to indulge in outdoor merrymaking with
some hunting thrown in. When this first started as an annual
event in the Forest is not clear; some say it began with the
Forest Charter of Henry III in 1226. There is no written record
that such a grant was ever made in any charter. Fisher, who
searched the City records, could find no documentary evidence
for this in Essex. It is more probable that permission for the
citizens of London to hunt on the king's waste was granted more
as a royal favour, even just a verbal one. However, during the
eighteenth and nineteenth centuries, many sporting licences
were granted by the Chief Justice of the Forest for the shooting
or taking of all the beasts of forest, chase and warren, except the
king's deer. A more picturesque, though doubtful, origin of civic

hunting goes back to the time of Richard I. It was the Easter custom in those days for the City apprentices to hunt the Jews through the streets of London, in a brutal kind of sport to satisfy high spirits. A certain rich Jew was willing to offer a large sum of money to the king if he would put an end to this, but insisted that the money would not be paid until such Jew-baiting was abolished. With an eye to the money the Lionheart agreed, but the citizens objected. So, to appease them, and that he might not be dubbed a spoilsport, the sovereign granted a royal favour: 'We of our Royal bounty grant them our goodly Forest of Epping as a hunting ground, yea, and yearly a stag of ten for their chase that shall try their speed better than ever yet did any dog Jew, though he, too, ran for his life.'

At all events hunting of the Forest deer among the civilian population became an established custom. In contrast to the stately splendour of the colourful royal hunts and the excellent seats of the experienced members of the retinue, the civic dignitaries in more sombre dress must at times have appeared ludicrous on, or rather off, their unaccustomed places in the saddle. It seems that the attempt of the City fathers to emulate their superiors in the days of Elizabeth caused some ridicule at court. On one occasion the queen offered the City three fee bucks annually in place of the Easter Chase. The Lord Mayor and his Commonalty, jealous of their rights and pleasure whether legal or not, rejected this offer. So the Easter Chase continued to flourish through the reign of the Stuarts and Hanoverians, more by favour or perhaps oversight of the successive monarchs.

The origin of the so-called Epping Hunt of the eighteenth and nineteenth centuries is believed to be a continuation of the much older Easter Chase, which used to be held in the various chases around London. The Epping Hunt, a more localised affair, met on the slopes overlooking Fairmead Bottom just below High Beech, where until recently there stood a fine old oak tree which could be seen from the main London–Epping new road. Every Easter Monday the citizens of London, in particular its cockneys, met by the old Fairmead oak. It was a day of merrymaking and

Page 69 (*above*) Branded commoner's beast showing the Manor of Waltham mark; (*below*) original marking iron for the Manor of Waltham

*Page 70* (*above*) Red deer stags, the original royal beasts, fighting during the rut; (*below*) the fox, a frequent Forest visitor, often seen in daylight

feasting, a Londoners' holiday in fact. The actual 'chase' was incidental to the meeting, and finally degenerated into a farce, especially when the last of the wild red deer were removed to Windsor Forest in the early part of the last century. Citizens came to show off their finery, to pickpocket, to enjoy the open air, to feast and to drink, and the more serious to try and hunt.

No official City hunts were held after 1807, and in that year the office of Master of the City Hounds, known as Mr Common Hunt—a probable abbreviation of the Commonalty's Huntsman—was abolished; a note to that effect appeared in *The Times*. Shortly afterwards the last of the wild Epping Forest deer was hunted by the well-known 'Tommy' Rounding, the chief huntsman of the Lord Warden, the Hon Wellesley Pole, of Wanstead. On 20 October 1827, after a good run, the stag was killed at West Ham. After that the Easter Day meeting, in which a carted stag was used, became a rowdy scene on Fairmead, as described by Tom Hood, in 'red coats, green coats, blue coats and black coats, sporting coats, sweeps with no coats', all arriving 'in coach and chaise, whisky and cart, gig and waggon, hunter and hack, horse and ass . . .' A huge crowd would gather and spread itself across the plain, consisting of 'baronets, butchers, dandies, huntsmen and dustmen, knifegrinders, tinkers and tailors, nobocracy and snobocracy . . .' The wretched stag, covered in ribbons, was brought across by cart from Buckhurst Hill to Fairmead and released. In terror it leaped away through the crowds, or it calmly made a bee-line for its home paddock behind the 'Bald Faced Stag'. The result was that few even saw it. In 1858, the Easter Hunt meeting officially ended; the head of the stag killed in that year may be seen hanging in the City's Guildhall.

And so the scene of a bawdy, brawling, annual concourse ended as an anti-climax to all the years of spectacular and noble hunting in the Kinge's Forrest. Today the place of such meetings is taken by the itinerant fairs which gather each bank holiday on the open spaces of Wanstead Flats and Chingford Plain.

# 4

# THE COMMONERS AND
# THEIR RIGHTS

Wee saye and present, that time out of mind, all persons
inhabiting within the Forest of Waltham, which have right of
Commoninge bye theire lands, messuages or tenemants, have
had common of pasture upon the said Forrest and waste Soyle
with all Commonable cattell.

From the Regard Roll in the Chancery Court Proceedings,
a Presentiment made by the Regarders of the Forest at the
Swainmote held at Stratford, 14 September 1630

The common rights of man to the land he lives on go back to
antiquity, but one thing seems certain: they were never granted
by any law, and may even antedate the existence of any private
land ownership. Today, however, all commonland lies in
someone's hands, whether at government level or by a single
individual. From what was once an entire kingdom owned by a
sovereign, land has been divided up between counties, hundreds,
vills, manors, castles and churches, until today the individual can
look upon his own modest freehold suburban home and garden
as his private castle and messuage. But, and it is an important
but, the right of common can still be enjoyed in many places in
Britain even today. It is up to the commoners themselves to
exercise their recognised right and to fight any opposition to
suppress it.

It was just this kind of threat to their livelihood which brought
on the climax to the history of Epping Forest in the last century
(see page 41). One of the commoners' most cherished rights was

72

that of pasturing their animals on the open 'waste'. At one time this right of 'common of pasture' presented no problem, but when the Royal Hunting Forests were created and laws made to protect the vert and venison, many restrictions were imposed on the movements of people and cattle. Firstly, although cattle pasturing was recognised by the Crown, the owners were not permitted to act as herdsmen. No 'staff herding', as it was called, was allowed, since the presence of humans would have kept the deer away from areas occupied by cattle. Consequently the farm animals would get the best feed. As a result the cattle strayed over all parts of the Forest, from manor to manor, known as 'intercommonage'. Such free-range cattle were controlled by the agisters so that they did not compete with the deer. Secondly, during the Fence Month between 21 June and 21 July, all cattle were removed from the Forest so as to leave the deer in peace and freedom to drop their young. The Fence Month law reads: 'It is defended and forbidden that anie man dwelland within the wood, or anie other sall enter within the close or haie parts of the Wood, with their beasts or cattell; be fifteen days before the Feast of St John the Baptist [6 July], and be fifteen days after the said feast, under paine and unlaw of aucht kye [cows].' Any animals not removed were impounded during this period, and after seven days were sold by auction at one of the markets at Epping, Waltham Abbey or Romford. Here and there can still be seen the broken-down remains of wooden pounds intended for holding straying cattle.

To recognise ownership, all cattle were branded with special parish marks. This was the job of the reeves who were sworn in at the Forest courts. Letters ran from A to R, but without regard to the geographical position of each parish. Cattle were then branded with the letter of the parish from which they were enlarged. When this practice first began is not known, but it is interesting to find that there is a cross in the brand mark above the A for Waltham and the Q for Wanstead. These properties belonged to the great monasteries of Waltham and Barking respectively. Fisher suggests that branding must therefore have existed before the Dissolution in the time of Henry VIII. Marking took place five times a year, in March, May, July, September and November. Today it is applied with heated tar placed on the marking iron. Commonable animals were referred to as 'horsebeasts' (horses) and 'neat beasts' (oxen, cows, calves and bullocks). They were either 'couchant' or 'levant', that is, they remained in one area or roamed through the Forest.

Sheep and goats were still further restricted, and usually kept on enclosed pasture or lawns away from the forest waste, because they tainted the ground over which the deer refused to feed. Such pastures were probably in existence as feeding areas attached to each vill long before the forest laws came into use. Even so, the commoners had to give way to the Crown because, it was said, of the dislike 'which the redd and falowe Deare doe naturally take of the sent [scent] and smell of sheepe, that do hurt and spoyle the covert, and thereby prejudice and wrong the Deare both in their feeding and layer [rest]'. Geese were also prohibited to stray.

However, the Dissolution of the monasteries by Henry VIII released large tracts of land from private ownership and, since there was a great demand for wool, sheep farming seemed a more profitable living than soil tilling. The commoners took full advantage of this, and in consequence the Forest was heavily overstocked with sheep. The courts were fully occupied in fining culprits who pastured sheep on forest land. Some argued that the peaceful sheep actually quietened the deer, and that they would even feed together, in spite of what was officially said to the contrary. This is debatable, but what was more serious was the competition for the same food—grass—which would arise between sheep and deer. Here again is a hint of wisdom in the policy of deer conservation laid down by the Normans, who realised that the habitat needed as much protection as the deer themselves. Over the past 300 years no sheep have been enlarged on Epping Forest soil.

Whereas all rights claimed on Royal Forest soil were normally only permitted by the Justice Seat, the right of 'common of pasture' was not required by law. Equally treasured by the common folk was the right of pannage—the free range of pigs which fed on acorns, roots and beech-mast. In so doing, the swine probably benefited the soil by acting as mobile ploughers and fertilisers as they grubbed through the leaf-mould. However, all pigs had to be ringed, and were only allowed on the forest wastes from fifteen days before to fifteen days after Michaelmas (4 September to 8 November), when the fruit would be on the ground.

For this 'priuilege' the owners paid a penny per animal as fee. Although the Anglo-Saxons were great swine-keepers, the Domesday survey lists only 774 swine for the nineteen Forest vills which were under the control of the reeves. However, from such records which would indicate the presence of oak trees, it appears that at one time there were extensive woodlands stretching beyond Epping as far as Brentwood. Much of this land today is arable, with only scattered woods in between. Pigs were not marked, but were turned out 'at ley', that is, at liberty; since there was a charge for this, and it was of benefit to the owners, both commoners and Crown were happy with the bargain. Pigs were handy units when it came to providing a daughter with a dowry.

The collecting of dues or rentals for the agistment of cattle and pigs, as it was called, was carried out by four agisters to each forest. The right of a commoner to turn out cattle was measured by the size of his holding, and thus the number of animals which he could support during the so-called winter heyning when animals were brought in. This was usually worked out by the Court of Attachment, and based on the value of the rental or the rating of the commoner's property. A 1790 order gives two cows or one horse for every £4 rental per annum. The reeves, in a charitable act, usually allowed poor cottagers with families to support the same right without payment. This helped towards preserving the privileges of every family in the parish in taking advantage of the right of 'common of pasture'. This ancient practice of pasturing animals goes back in records to the eighth century, when reference is made to it by Ethelbald, who ruled Mercia (716–57). Today, some 1,200 years later, the commoners' cattle still wander freely through the Forest.

Turning next to the equally important right of lopwood, this concerns the use of Forest wood and timber for fuel, carpentry and building, in days when alternative materials were non-existent. At a later date the timber was prized for use in building wooden ships, and at one stage was the government's excuse for trying to sell off the Forest trees (see page 37). The right to lop a tree, that is, to remove the branches, goes back to antiquity, and was practised by everyone as a normal birthright. Then, as with the right of commonage, the law stepped in when the royal forests were created and imposed its restrictions. This was again designed to benefit the deer or the Crown. For example, to keep lopping under control, the law forbad the cutting of trees or underwood without licence from the Forest official called the woodward. Even in Canute's day 'none shall touch our wood and underwood without the licensing of the chief men of the Forest; whoever does so shall be guilty of a breach of the Royal Chase. But if any cut an oak or other tree which bears fruit for the deer, he shall besides pay 20s. to the King'.

In this way the use of vert was controlled. 'Special vert' applied to the fruit-bearing trees of value to the deer, such as the wild pear, crab, hawthorn, cherry and holme (holly). Any person claiming right to cut Forest timber had to leave such fruit-trees alone. Indeed, the woodwards who controlled the timber could claim on behalf of the king this 'browst', as it was named, as winter feed for the deer. Stealing such browst was a serious matter; the offender had to pay for its value, and might even have to forfeit his cart and horse. Trees were classified according to height. Tallwood consisted of normal trees which were preserved for their timber. Short tallwood probably referred to the trees whose branches had been lopped for firewood. Trees and bushes below 6ft were Crown property and intended as food for the deer. The woodward who controlled all this was also in charge of any private land which came within the forested area. In such a case the owner was obliged to appoint a woodward who then answered to the owner in all cases of trespass or injury to the vert. At the same time, being a Crown official who swore fidelity to the king, the woodward had to answer to the sovereign in respect of offences against venison.

If an owner did not swear an oath to abide by the forest laws, then his wood could be confiscated. In this case there was a chance to appeal before the Justice Seat, but if this were not done within a year and a day, then the seized land remained in the hands of the Crown. One odd feature of the right to property was the interpretation put upon a waste, that is, open Crown land. If illegal felling had been committed, then, as Fisher explains, if one stood on the stump of a felled oak and could see or regard five or more felled trees within sighting distance, then the area was declared a waste, and could technically be taken by the Crown. Either that, or a punishment was imposed by a fine.

Inspection of private woods within forest confines was made from time to time by twelve knights, called a 'regard'. In the Patent Roll of Henry III there are listed twelve 'chapters of the Regard'. These gave the findings of the regarders during their tour of duty. For example, the knights counted the number of 'eyries of hawks and falcons', the 'nests of honey', the amount of 'herbage in the King's demesne', the amount of 'removal of timber', the number of 'forges, mines and other diggings', and so on. It is interesting to note, under the thirteenth heading of the Forest Charter of 1217, that 'every Freeman shall have, within his own woods, ayries of Hawks, Sparrow-hawks, Faulcons, Eagles and Herons; and shall have also the Honey that is found within the woods'.

Apart from land ownership, whether private or royal, the right of lopwood was jealously guarded by the commoners. This was carried out in wintertime when the sap had fallen. The Essex commoners in the Loughton Manor used to carry out this ancient right by insisting that this had been confirmed for them by Queen Elizabeth I. They would assemble on Staples Hill behind the old town of Loughton, or Lucton, on the evening of

All Saints' Day (11 November) and celebrate the occasion by lighting a bonfire and drinking ale. Then, at the stroke of midnight, the axemen would set to work for an hour or so, lopping off the branches. At 2 am they would return home to bed. Lopping could then continue until St George's Day (23 April). To maintain their right of lopwood the commoners had to perform this ceremony each year.

It is said that, on one occasion, the Lord of the Manor of Waltham invited the commoners into his home for the lopping celebration, as a ruse to terminate their rights. He quietly locked the doors and bolted the windows as they were merrymaking, so as to prevent lopping at the appointed hour. But the wily villagers, suspecting something of this kind, had left some of their comrades outside. They were able to smash in the doors and windows when the time arrived, and so all could reach the woods. One method of lopping was to pollard a tree, that is, to decapitate it, leaving a bare trunk standing. This was carried out at a 6ft height, about the length of an average man and his axe. Only the larger branches were removed, leaving the smaller ones for future lopping. The result must have presented a strange sight where a whole area of hornbeams, oaks or beeches would have resembled a stark battlefield of bare trunks with hardly any cover. In time, if carefully done, a pollarded tree will grow further branches but in a bunched up fashion from a common crown. An experiment to see the result of such treatment was carried out by the conservators in 1952. A number of oaks were pollarded in a grove called Woodman's Glade, just behind Chingford Plain. Although some of the trees died from fire, others are still standing and have grown bushy tops to the old trunks.

If a tree was spoiled or became diseased (it was then called a starveling), the dead timber went to the manor lord. Lopped branches were cleaned or brashed of side shoots, which were left on the ground for the deer to eat. The branches were then cut into 6ft lengths and drawn away on a sledge made of a frame of wood shod with iron. Wood collected in this manner was the property of the commoner who gathered it, but it was not to be sold. Further privileges carried out by the commoners included the catching of fish from common waters (called piscary), the gathering of kindling (fallen branches called estovers) and the collecting of bracken (fernery) as bedding for cattle. These activities would have caused little disturbance to the wild animals, but no doubt they were under the watchful eye of the regarder. Turbary—the gathering of turf or peat used for fuel or roofing—was probably a minor practice in Waltham Forest at one time.

# 5

# FOREST MANAGEMENT

Everyone who aspires to be a forester should exercise his
imagination. He works for posterity. It is essential for his
success that he should, with full knowledge of natural processes,
have ever present in his mind the probable results of his
operations, not only in this generation, but fifty or a hundred
years hence.

EDWARD NORTH BUXTON

To carry out those functions entrusted to them, the City Corporation have appointed an Epping Forest and Open Spaces
Committee comprising twelve members elected from the Court
of Common Council and four verderers elected by the commoners. These meet regularly and advise on Forest matters. The
work of maintenance and order is carried out by a staff of keepers
and woodmen under the superintendent. The superintendent
resides at The Warren, a country house just below Loughton,
converted from a former inn called 'The Reindeer'. To it are
attached offices for the administrative staff, also buildings for the
necessary equipment of tools, tractors, saws, etc used in modern
forestry. The only other office is that held by the reeves who
mark the cattle as they are enlarged on the Forest each year. This
privilege is still exercised by a number of commoners, usually
farmers, but is the right of anyone who in any of the Forest
parishes is the owner of, at minimum, half an acre of land ex-
clusive of the site of his house. This entitles him to own and
enlarge 'two beasts [cattle] or one horse'. In a number of cases
such common rights have been disqualified and or/quieted in
title.

Each keeper sees to it that the bye-laws are not infringed. Order is maintained more by persuasion than by prosecution. On the whole there is little damage to trees and wildlife which can be called deliberate, and the Forest may still be regarded as a valuable nature sanctuary on the doorstep of a great metropolis. This, however, poses problems in terms of people. The two main and somewhat unpleasant tasks of the keepers are the clearance of litter left by visitors—and even at times deliberately dumped by cars and lorries—and the occasional illegal use of firearms. Sometimes, too, molestation may occur, and can lead to a court case. It must be admitted that there is always some risk to women and children who enter the thicket areas in the neighbourhood of convenient roadways. They could become victims of maladjusted individuals, though this rarely happens away from the roads and built-up areas. The author has frequently spent whole nights roaming the Forest depths without seeing a soul, save the wild deer, fox and badger. The heart of Epping Forest is probably a far safer place at night than some of London's streets.

When the conservators took over the Forest in 1878, much of it was in a sorry state. Persistent lopping at short intervals, whether by means of pollarding, or by coppicing (cutting down to a stump from which new branches grow), had resulted in an abundance of stunted growth, restricted in girth, overcrowded and gnarled in appearance. Many trees were hollow and in a state of decay, a condition which can still be seen today in some specimens. To maintain a 'natural aspect to the Forest' the conservators had first to recreate the more natural tree growth. One way to do this is by removing all the old and distorted trees, and then to 'plant up' the denuded area with seedlings, as is practised in normal forestry. This would have resulted in a certain amount of regimentation with trees all of the same age, and a need to enclose with fencing for protection against attacks by deer and other animals, including humans. Damage to fencing foiled this attempt at regeneration and was abandoned because of expense.

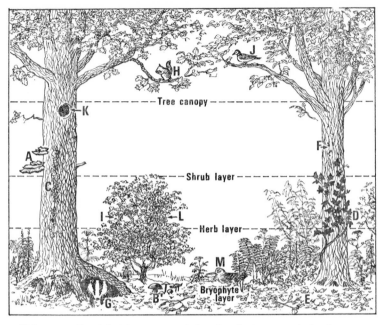

[The woodland habitat: growth levels of plants and the homes of some animals. Plants: A parasite (bracket fungus); B saprophyte (toadstool); C epiphyte (lichen); D climber (ivy). Animals: E leaf mould (litter fauna); F under bark (beetle grub); G below ground (badger); H in tree (squirrel); I in bush (dormouse); J on branch (woodpigeon); K in tree trunk (woodpecker); L in bush (song thrush); M on ground (woodcock)

The policy today is to rely on natural regeneration, letting nature provide the seedlings for successive growth. Sometimes this may fail because of grazing animals eating the young growth. To prevent this an alternative method has been tried out with limited success. When an area is felled, the branches and 'brashwood' are left to lie as cover for the growing seedlings. Even so the deer and squirrels have sometimes managed to penetrate. In some areas the nature of the soil has inhibited germination. Generations of semi-decayed and impacted leaves lying on cold London Clay have in a number of places formed a hard, acid podsol in which germination is arrested. Attempts at breaking up this kind of soil with a disc harrow, thereby letting in air and rainwater, have improved conditions. At one time the task of breaking up the leaf-litter was performed by the commoners' pigs as they rooted for acorns and beech mast. Before this the herds of deer, wild pigs and cattle helped to keep the soil loose.

This encouragement of regeneration by natural means is a slow business. Even by hand-planting, a forester does not expect to see a mature crop for many years to come, perhaps not even in his lifetime. Eventually, if the Forest still stands in, say, fifty or a hundred years from now, the 'natural aspect' for which the conservators are striving will have been fully achieved. Meanwhile, and for the past ninety years, dead and dying pollards have gradually been removed and natural growth allowed to take their place. In the early days when there was a high density of pollarded and coppiced trees standing in close intimacy, it was first necessary to thin out here and there. Old and diseased pollards were removed entire, and with coppiced trees all save one or two branches arising from the old stump cut away. These adventitious branches, as they are termed, whether arising from a coppiced stool or from the crown of a pollard, have since grown to such a height that in some places today they resemble fully grown trees with a closed-in canopy above them. This so-called 'false high forest' presents a far more natural aspect than that which faced the conservators when they took over their task. New trees are flourishing, and will in time replace the old pollards. It is perhaps this mixture of ancient and modern—the old pollards intermingled with the vigorous young growth, from seedling upwards—which gives the present Forest its character and variety.

In between the stands of trees, in many parts of the Forest, are open patches consisting of glades where felling has been carried out, or what are quite probably the original grazing areas or 'lawns' situated around the old forest vills. This more open aspect, more in the nature of an accepted common for grazing, is to be found in the southern part of the Forest, at Wanstead and Leytonstone Flats, also at Chingford Plain which fell to the plough during the selling of Forest land in the last century. The plough furrows can still be seen. To relieve the monotony of a continuous closed-in forest of mature trees, the conservators are attempting to preserve these open spaces. All this takes time and money, especially the grubbing up of bushes and young trees which are slowly invading the glades. At one time the animals performed a valuable role in keeping open the grazing areas. It is perhaps not generally realised what a difference some wild animals, even domesticated ones, can make to a countryside. Deer, cattle, sheep and rabbits are all grass feeders and will also browse on young growth, so they may be described as natural landscape gardeners, apart from being mobile fertilisers, as they roam about the Forest. I remember bringing something of this sort to the hearing of the parliamentary committee when invited as a witness to point out the value of grazing animals in keeping down the undergrowth in open spaces. This was during an attempt, which failed, to amend the Epping Forest Act by restricting the movement of Forest cattle (it was even suggested that they should be tethered), owing to the nuisance they were causing to motorists and gardeners. The animals are not dairy stock, but beef cattle used to roaming about after the fashion of North American prairie herds. It was feared that tethering them might also lead to some misguided people using them as targets for sticks and stones.

Ponds, too, provide a pleasant contrast to a Forest walk, helping to break up the monotony of trees. They are an object of interest to the naturalist, and of importance as small nature reserves containing a world of water life.

All this variety of woodland, glade, heath and pond requires considerable attention and maintenance by the conservators who try to preserve it. Without man's interference nature would in due course level out the landscape by filling it up entirely with trees. A glade, for instance, will in time become overgrown with scrub, then the young trees will push through to close up the gap. With ponds, the water space is slowly invaded by the fringing reeds or rushes, and filled with sediment and plant remains, on which ultimately grass, then trees, may grow. Today there are not enough cattle or deer, and no sheep as formerly, to keep the spaces open. The only places where the grass grows short is where there are regular gatherings of visitors. Constant trampling may even wear away the vegetation, and this is often how paths originate. In accessible places, such as the roadside verges or village greens, local councils help the City Corporation by employing workmen to cut the grass with mechanical mowers. The deeper forest glades can only be kept open by periodic thinning. Some assistance in this has been given privately, and by young volunteers of the Conservation Corps of the Council for Nature. The larger Forest ponds are dredged at intervals of a few years so as to remove excessive plant growth and decaying leaves. In tree-thinning, note is always taken of well-developed trees around which a clearance is made to let in light and 'elbow room'; this also applies to the sturdier pollards and rare trees. The first trees to be felled are usually the birch and beech, of which there are still plenty. The birch is a rapid coloniser and the beech regenerates freely from seed. Trees needing protection include the crab-apple, maple, wild cherry and wild service. These are scattered throughout the Forest, but nowhere in great numbers. Thorn bushes, such as briar and bramble, sloe and hawthorn, are allowed to grow unchecked as roadside and border plants, but may require thinning where they threaten a glade. Oddly enough this kind of scrub growth is of advantage to certain animals and plants which need some cover as a retreat or for hiding. A fallow doe will resort to a thick bracken-covered glade to drop its fawn. A nightingale will nest on the ground under the safety of thorn bushes, and the adder will use them as a retreat from danger. Thickets of holly, dense in places and slow to spread, are usually left alone as this is favourite shelter and food for the deer, especially in winter.

In the initial stages of Forest maintenance, partly under pressure from the public, the conservators attempted to remove dead and fallen trees, and to carry out drainage where the ground remained waterlogged. This is no longer the policy, since a fallen tree and a boggy patch of ground can attract interesting and sometimes unusual bog and epiphytic plant life. This is of interest to the naturalist, and natural history is, after all, one of the amenities of the Forest. Indeed, a happy relationship exists between the conservators and the naturalists, both of whom are concerned with preserving wildlife. The more natural the Forest can be, the better the chances of survival of its animals and plants. Buxton writes:

> It goes without saying that in a natural forest we should preserve those features which are not of man's doing. As an instance of this may be mentioned the importance of retaining trees which are decaying, trees which are dead, trees which have been overthrown by the forces of nature, as well as those which are full of vigour. Such features are the characteristics of all virgin woodlands. Our Forest is also a document of nature with its tale to tell. The failures, its ruins, should be preserved, as well as its vigorous growth. It should not be trimmed and garnished.

The scars of the Forest which existed in Buxton's day, such as straight-sided plantations, gravel diggings, straight-cut rides and ditches in place of winding streams and footpaths, have today been rectified by judicious felling and thinning so that the contours of borders and pathways have been softened and the watercourses restored to their former meanderings. Far from being eyesores the old gravel pits have turned out in many places to be objects of real beauty, and now support a wealth of pondlife.

Page 87 (*above*) Badger boar emerging from its sett; (*below*) five-toed snow track of the badger

Page 88 (*above*) Grey squirrel, first introduced into the Forest in the 1930s; (*below*) woodmouse with young, a common nocturnal Forest mammal

# 6

# THE EPPING FOREST DEER

Near the Ley spreads out a chase of vast extent, full of game, the largest and fattest deer in the Kingdom; called heretofore, by way of eminence, the Forest of Essex, now Waltham Forest, from the town of Waltham, in Saxon Wealdham, ie a dwelling in the woods.

written by Camden, the historian (late sixteenth century)

Three species of deer once lived in Waltham Forest—the red, the roe and the fallow. Of these the last still survives in present-day Epping Forest, but is rapidly diminishing in numbers. Attempts are being made to save this herd because of its historic associations and unique position among the fauna in Britain. These are truly wild animals and of an unusual dark colouring.

One's first impression of a fallow deer is of a pretty, light brown or fawn coloured creature, neatly dappled in white. This is the typical form of the semi-tame deer which are scattered throughout the country in parks and paddocks. They resemble the ancestral species, *Dama dama*, originating in the countries of the Eastern Mediterranean, in Asia Minor. Whereas the park deer sometimes contain dark specimens, they never seem to be as black as the Forest deer. Even the fawns are of this colouring. An occasional paler, even white, animal has occurred at times in the past; this has probably been due to some contamination from outside, as stray park deer could have wandered in. It has been the practice of the conservators in the past to destroy such animals, so as to preserve the purity of this ancient melanic breed.

F                                            89

The melanic feature, a possible dominant in colour varieties, may have been passed down from some ancestral strain, of which we have no knowledge. All that is known about such dark animals is that James I, in 1612, imported some from Norway into Scotland, from which a number were taken into the New Forest and Epping Forest. This also appears to be the earliest historic record of imported fallow deer. However, fallow are known to have existed in Britain at a much earlier date and were definitely here by Norman times. Perhaps the Phoenicians brought them over when they came to trade; or it may have been the Danes, who were keen huntsmen. There is no mention of deer introductions by the Romans.

The fossil record contains many finds of red and roe deer, both indigenous to Britain, and hunted by Stone Age man. Remains have been found in Pleistocene deposits along the Thames valley and its tributaries. At one stage, during the mild interglacial period, there also existed along the Thames a large form of fallow deer, named *Dama clactoniana* after the well-known fossil locality on the Essex coast. This appears to have died out, and does not occur during or after the last Ice Age. Instead only the red and roe returned as the ice retreated, taking the place of the reindeer. From this it is presumed that the fallow deer in Britain today, whether park-reared or wild, is an introduction from the Mediterranean.

Deer comprise a family of cloven-hoofed animals noted for their grace and beauty. The slender legs, with very elongated 'hands' and 'feet', each ending in a pair of hoofed 'fingers' and 'toes', are adapted for swift movement and speedy flight from danger. The senses of sight, hearing and smell are acute, so that approach is difficult. Their constant alertness enables them to detect and avoid an enemy by instant flight. To this the wild deer in Britain owe much of their survival from previous natural enemies, such as wolf and bear. Since the extermination of these two carnivores, deer have become the quarry exclusively of man.

After centuries of pursuit, the wild Forest deer still retain their shyness and suspicion of humans. Walking quietly through the

Forest, one suddenly becomes aware of some alert forms standing motionless beneath the trees, almost invisible in their dark coats were it not for the constant twitching of ears and tails. Heads are upraised and turned towards the intruder. Unless under cover in some ambush, I have never been able to approach the deer undetected. What usually happens is that there is a sudden thrashing noise in the undergrowth, and one catches a glimpse of a leaping form or two bounding away to disappear in seconds. If the going is more open and the encounter more distant, then the retreat is more orderly, provided that one stands still or approaches slowly. Their restlessness is very apparent; it is the habit of fallow deer to move in jerky motion, ears twitching and tails wagging. Like horses and cattle, they are plagued by flies in warm weather. At first they stand motionless, heads raised, but there are signs of nervousness in all their little movements. False alarms cause one to start away jerkily, another to leap sideways. There may be a lot of jostling and bunching, as if the group is eager to set off, yet none will take the lead. Signs of imminent flight are the sudden movements of the head as it moves sharply back and forward. Finally, the threat of danger is too close, usually at about 30yd. A leader, often a mature doe, breaks away at a trot and the rest immediately follow in sheep-like fashion at a sharp trot. If no danger follows they stop a little way off and the whole business of bunching, and ear and tail twitching is resumed. When hotly pursued by, say, a dog, the deer stream off at a gallop. When really alarmed they may progress with tremendous leaps of 15ft or more. One curious progress is made by bouncing along on all four legs held out stiffly in what is termed 'buck-jumping'.

Deer are described as social animals, living in parties or herds. This is certainly noticeable among park deer which tend to keep together, due perhaps to restriction of space. In the open Forest they associate in groups, so that counting them, a yearly practice, is not so easy. Annually the keepers go out with the first fall of snow to estimate the number of deer within their respective beats, and similar counts are carried out by amateur societies, such as the Essex Field Club and the Deer Society. From this it would appear that few deer exist inside the actual Forest boundaries these days, and must be looked for in the quieter corners. The most likely places to see them are in the northern parts, in Epping Thicks among the hollies, and on the north-western borders between Woodredon Farm and the Copt Hall estate. There are a number of outlying lanes and woods in this area, to which the deer have resorted for greater security. The constant pressure and disturbance of recent years has caused the herd to spread out more, but it still remains faithful to the Forest, and a number return there for the winter months.

Causes for the decline in numbers of this unique black herd are complex. Poaching, the chasing and killing of fawns by dogs, accidents when crossing a road are among the main types of casualty. Mortality among deer can be high at times, even in a park herd, especially among the yearlings following a wet summer. This could be due to the wet grass, a condition loosely known as 'scouring', or perhaps from a parasitic condition. It was stated by the chronicler in 1489 and in 1493 that '316 red and fallow deere' were found 'dede of murrayn in the Forest'. Murrein was a general term in those days for any number of internal complaints, some of which could have been caused by parasitic worms.

Fallow deer stand about 3ft at the withers, and weigh on average 10–12 stone. The male or buck carries antlers which grow afresh each year. In fallow the full 'attire'—that is, full antler growth—is reached in the fifth year. Each pair of antlers is shed annually from the pedicels, two bony outgrowths from the frontal bones of the skull. When fresh antlers grow out they are covered in a soft, furry skin, the 'velvet'. This protects the growing antlers and supplies food through a rich flow of blood. The antler surface is grooved to take the blood vessels. A process of hardening or ossification progresses from the pedicels to the antler tips, and at the same time the velvet dries and flakes off.

Antlers commence growth immediately after the previous

pair are shed, usually in May in the adults, and in June in juveniles. Growth is complete by August, and the velvet is rubbed off against tree trunks and branches by the end of the month. At first they look clean and white, but later turn darker with weathering and use. Antlers first appear in the second year of life, each a simple prong a few inches long. The youngster is called a pricket. In the third year, brow and tray tines appear with the beam above showing signs of palmation. In successive years the palmation increases with more points appearing until full growth is attained in about the fifth year. Shed antlers are seldom found in the Forest. They soon become buried in the leaf litter and ditches, and many are gnawed by the deer themselves. It is suggested that they do this to make up a calcium deficiency in their diet.

Compared with park deer, the Forest animals are of inferior size, and a mature buck carries a much smaller 'head' of antlers. In one exceptional case, a buck in a Sussex deer park had antlers 37in long, 3in across the beam, and carried thirty-five points or spellers. In a Forest buck a good head is about 20in long with beam width of 2in, and about twenty points. Poor feeding as well as constant in-breeding may account for the inferior quality. As William Twici, huntsman to Edward II, wrote, 'The head [antlers] of deer grow according to the pasture, good or otherwise.'

A typical day in the life of the wild fallow deer is not easy to follow due to their shyness. A party will be out feeding at dawn in one of the fields bordering the Forest; the area under observation by the author was in the fields between Theydon Bois and Debden Green before it was taken over for camping activities. By about 10 am, if not disturbed before then, the party would retire to rest in some secluded hollow or thicket. The party might then return for a second feed of grass in the afternoon, and perhaps a third one in the evening before dusk, especially in the summer. In autumn and winter the grazing appeared to be more continuous as the herd moved slowly through the Forest, eating grass, gathering acorns, crab apples and toadstools. Fallow will also feed on young leaves and buds, and in spring it is possible to see where branch tips have been torn away during browsing. The reason why deer will feed, then retire, at regular intervals, is a means of survival handed down from the days when these timid creatures had enemies such as wolf and bear to avoid. Dawn and dusk in the open are reasonably safe places and times in which to feed away from danger, and an enemy approach is quickly noticed. Many times the author has attempted to crawl towards feeding deer, but with little success.

Since deer are ruminants, like cattle, they 'chew the cud'. Food, such as grass, is first hastily cropped and swallowed. Then, on retirement, the resting animal is hidden from enemies and protected from the hot sun as it ruminates. Half-digested food is regurgitated in small lumps, the 'cud', then chewed thoroughly with the strong grinding teeth and swallowed a second time for final digestion. Canines are missing in most deer, as in cattle, and in the front the chisel or incisor teeth grow only in the lower jaw. These bite the food against a hard pad in the upper jaw. Unlike horses and sheep, however, deer usually tear away their food with the aid of the tongue.

Teeth marks of fallow can sometimes be found on the bark of trees, especially the holly. This is where the lower incisors have scraped away vertical grooves of the bark. The preference for holly bark has been a feature of the Forest herd which the author first noticed in the early 1930s. I thought this was caused by male deer rubbing their antlers against trees to clean off the velvet. Then, one day, I was lucky in seeing a deer scraping off the bark with up and down movements of its head.

The yearly cycle of a fallow deer's activities also follows a certain pattern. Sexes begin to mingle by summer's end as the mating or rutting season begins. The bucks are then in full condition for fighting and mating, and start to gather in the does, being polygamous. The collecting and protecting of its harem is a more casual affair than with red deer, where fighting to the death has occurred. Fallow seem to indulge more in sparring matches and feats of strength. The two opposing master bucks

94

push against one another with locked antlers, turning in circles as they do so. This explains the curious circles of disturbed leaves and soil seen in certain parts of the Forest. The fighting of the buck suggests not so much a fight over wives as a claim for territory. At the height of the rut a curious moo-like grunt may be heard as the bucks call defiance. This is the time to step warily in the hopes of catching a glimpse of two rivals about to do battle. In places where the buck drinks, it may wallow in the mud, which is known as 'soiling'. The earth is trampled and pawed around the wallow, and even thrown about by the antlers.

As winter approaches, the parties tend to merge into larger groups, and in the past I have seen as many as sixty in one group, usually of both sexes and all ages. It is said that the bucks will stay apart in the winter, as in the case of red deer, but I have not noticed this in the Forest. In early June each expectant mother slips away on her own to some hidden retreat, such as a thick cover of bracken, in order to drop her fawn. This can happen early in a fallow doe's life, and she has been known to become a mother at two years. The buck usually takes about five years to become mature.

A doe will hide her baby for about a week, coming regularly to feed it. Then she leads it off to rejoin the main party. If disturbed, a mother will either hide her fawn, or lead it away to cover. One of my happiest memories of the Forest is that of a doe which leapt out of some bracken, turned and stood facing me a few yards off. She called and stamped her foot. I had stumbled on her fawn, half hidden in tall bracken where it lay motionless at my feet. The tiny mite, all legs and eyes, stared at me trustingly without twitching a muscle. Normally the fallow baby is heavily spotted as a means of camouflage, but this youngster was as dark as its parent. This was also the case with the only two still-born young I have seen. One, in fact, was removed from its mother who was killed on the road.

The most successful move in the preservation of the herd has been the making of a deer sanctuary. Through the support of the Buxton family, much of their estate at Birch Hall close to

Theydon Bois has been given over to this experiment. The land of open grass, a wood and a lake is now surrounded by a strong metal net fence. On the Forest side are a number of deer leaps. Each consists of two ramps rising towards one another with a gap between, through which the fence passes. In this manner a deer can run up one ramp, leap the fence, then run down the other, and can do so in either direction. Now that a sizeable party of deer is inside this sanctuary, and has actually started to breed, the deer leaps have been closed. It is hoped to build up the herd for eventual liberation; if this is not practicable, then it will remain imprisoned. A similar number of Forest deer are being kept at the country zoo at Whipsnade. At least, in this way, this famous herd will not die out, even though it may never again roam freely through the Kinge's Forrest as it has done for a thousand years.

# 7

# THE BADGER AND THE FOX

Apart from the fallow deer, there are other mammals living in the Forest, although their numbers have decreased somewhat in recent years. Mammals by and large are shy and elusive creatures, and tend to leave places where there is constant disturbance by humans. Down the ages they have come to mistrust people because of the manner in which they have been hunted and persecuted by them, either for food, sport, or for their skins. In the Forest there are bye-laws to protect them, but the stigma remains, and the very scent of man is a danger signal not to be ignored. A number of mammals have taken to night activities, when the danger is temporarily abated, and this is why some of them are practically unknown to humans, who are day animals. Most of us, for instance, would confess to some ignorance if asked about the badger, a noble and ancient Briton which has roamed our woodlands since prehistoric times. Brock, as he was known to our Saxon forebears, seldom emerges above ground until darkness settles.

My first encounter with badgers was an experience I shall never forget. It happened during my camping days with the Boy Scouts in the 1930s. We had a delightful camp site in a field bordering the Forest, near Debden Green beyond Loughton, a quiet backwater in those days seldom disturbed by visitors. A Forest keeper took me along to a badger sett one spring evening, then left me to myself perching in an old pollard hornbeam overlooking a freshly cleaned-out hole. My instructions were to remain quiet and patient until night had fallen and the Forest was stilled, keeping a close watch on the dark hole beneath my dangling feet. As the moon rose above the tree tops, black shadows spread over the leafy floor of this ancient woodland. A late blackbird was ending his evensong as the first owl made its call to the night. Gentle rustling of moving leaves in a soft breeze could be heard as the throb of traffic on the distant road died away, yet there was no wind. Could it be the rustle of tiny wood mice which are common enough in the Forest? And yet this sound was all around me, in the trees even. Only years later did I learn that I was listening to the champing of innumerable jaws as myriads of night-feeding caterpillars dined off the tree leaves, and the sound, like fine rain, of their droppings falling on to the dead leaves below.

Suddenly there was a sharp rustle, and there, in the black hole of the doorway, was a pointed head, sharply arrowed in white. For a moment I stared old Brock in the face, then he was gone. Had he caught my scent? Had I moved in my excitement? The thrill of the moment is something no badger watcher ever looses, and I was to see much more of this wonderful creature in the years to come.

Sometimes old Brock never appears. He is craftily scenting the air while still just below ground, catches a danger scent, then quietly retires. So the night's vigil is wasted. Or he may block the doorway and start his evening scratching. Badgers are very good at this. He may grunt and grumble a bit as his wife nudges him aside to put in an appearance. Is this why they are called boar and sow? A nearby tree or fallen log comes in useful to rub themselves against to cure an itch or for cleaning their claws. Next they visit the toilet, quite literally, since they never soil their homes. Somewhere in the vicinity will be found a group of shallow pits dug near the sett by these clean-living animals and used as latrines. On many an occasion I have collected samples of the dung for examination under the microscope. This sometimes reveals undigested food remains, and illustrates the wide range of their diet, such as plants, roots, insects, small mammals, and especially earthworms. Dr Ernest Neal, Britain's leading

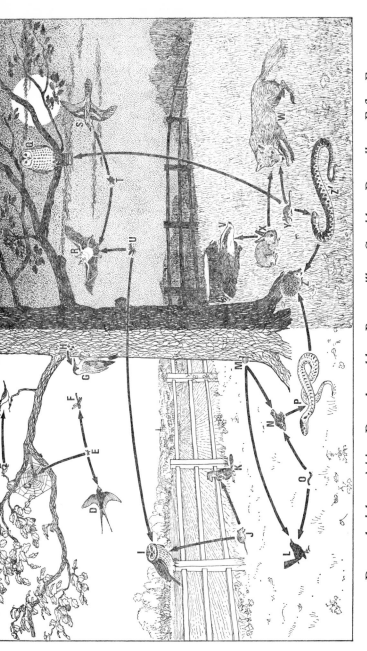

Day and night activities. Day: A warbler; B caterpillar; C spider; D swallow; E fly; F dragonfly; G woodpecker; H bark beetle; I small owl; J bank vole; K weasel; L blackbird; M snail; N frog; O earthworm; P grass snake. Night: Q tawny owl; R bat; S nightjar; T moth; U beetle; V badger; W fox; X rabbit; Y woodmouse; Z hedgehog; Z¹ adder authority on the badger, suggests that worms figure highly on its menu, and this is confirmed by the microscope. On the slide in a smear of dung may be seen numerous *setae*, the tiny spines embedded in a worm's skin.

The sett itself is under constant attention, and spring cleaning is an all-year-round affair. Piles of earth are heaped up before each entrance, and these are used in rotation. The front door is forsaken for the back door, so to speak. Along the shallower tunnels are air vents reaching the surface, so that the underground fortress is kept sweet and well ventilated. Side chambers leading off the lower tunnels are the sleeping quarters, cosily lined with grass or bracken, sometimes leaves, or even loose hay or straw from the farmer's field.

A used entrance to a sett, and there may be many openings, can be examined for unmistakable occupation in the form of loose hair which has caught up on a root. About 3in long, a badger hair looks greyish, but has a black band just behind the tip. In soft earth by the sett, or along the Forest rides, may be found the badger's footprints. The animal walks flat-footed—plantigrade—so that five toes are present; in front are the imprints of claws, and behind the broad kidney-shaped pad mark.

Sometimes in the piled-up soil from a freshly cleaned-out hole may be found bones and other animal remains. If these are of rabbit or chicken, then the hole has almost certainly been occupied by a fox. The musty smell should reveal his presence. Reynard is lazy by badger standards, and will make temporary use of part of a badger sett. Whereas a fox brings home his dinner, a badger eats it on the spot. There are times when I have waited for badger young to emerge, only to find myself watching some tumbling fox cubs which had been born in a badger's domain. Once I found the mutilated bodies of fox cubs at one Forest sett. The badgers had apparently resented the fox family's presence, and committed the crime of vulpicide.

Badgers have probably lived in the Forest for centuries, but little has been written about them. In 1880 Buxton introduced several pairs into Loughton Manor, and in 1899 they were reported to be entrenched in the ancient Forest camp in Monk Wood. In all, five setts have been occupied since I first became interested in the Forest badgers. During World War II they were severely decimated when the Ministry of Agriculture carried out a gassing campaign to exterminate foxes, in order to protect the neighbouring chicken farms whose eggs were so precious during the food rationing. Since foxes often occupy badger setts, most of the holes were gassed. Since then the badgers have recovered, and I knew of three setts in occupation during the post-war years. Latterly, however, they have again declined, partly due to the hazards of road traffic, partly to the electrification of the railway line to Epping, and maybe also because of too much badger-watching by over-enthusiastic naturalists!

By 1968 all setts appeared to be extinct, with the holes filling in or taken over by rabbits. A voluntary organisation called 'Wildlife Aid', based on the Westcliffe area in South Essex, then rescued a threatened family of badgers from a sett on the grounds of the North Thames Gas Board, where building extensions were to take place. A sow and three cubs were removed and later liberated in a deserted sett in Epping Forest, under the supervision of Fred Speakman. At the time of writing these animals seem to have settled in and may become the nucleus of a new colony of Forest badgers.

In contrast to the energetic and homely badger, the fox will not build a home if it can avoid doing so. It will take over and enlarge an existing burrow. As ancient a Briton as the badger, Reynard is much more in evidence in the Forest than its nocturnal neighbour. It is generally agreed among naturalists that the fox is really a day animal forced into darkness by centuries of persecution. In quiet and undisturbed places it can often be encountered in broad daylight, and I have frequently met it face to face in the Forest. The foxy colouring suggests a camouflage dress which would blend with the dead leaves of the Forest floor, the bracken and heather. Here is a refuge from the hunt. Recently the number of foxes have increased, coming closer into the built-up areas. The fox now raids the dustbins in suburbia and has taken to kennelling in some of the churchyards or cemeteries. On occasions it has penetrated as far as Wanstead Park, where I have found its neat trail of footprints in the snow. Residents of Woodford, Chingford and Loughton have seen the fox in their gardens. The situation is somewhat ironic. In spite of foxhunting, shooting, traps and poisons, the fox population is holding its own. The loss of a staple food such as the rabbit may have forced it more to our notice as it turns to chicken houses, dustbins and rubbish tips. It has even been known to kill and eat a cat or two in the Forest neighbourhood.

Possibly the fox's acute senses and intelligence has made it a successful match for man. I remember once passing through Monk Wood at dead of night, and hearing the familiar patter of a fox-trot through the dry beech leaves. Standing quite still and awaiting its approach, I heard it suddenly stop in its tracks. The wind was in my favour, so it could not smell me. There was no sound and my silhouette could have been mistaken for a tree trunk. Yet this wary animal had its suspicions. In a moment or so it made a complete detour around me, caught my scent from the rear, and hurried away. On another occasion, when the snow lay heavy in the Forest during the severe 1962–3 winter, I followed a fox trail for 5 miles, during which it visited a rabbit warren, a neighbouring chicken farm, crossed a frozen pond presumably in search of waterfowl, and even attempted to scratch open a potato clamp. The tracks at one stage showed an abortive attempt at catching a pheasant. This was a single night's travel, at the end of which a very hungry fox returned home.

# 8

# OTHER MAMMALS

Apart from the fox and badger, Forest carnivores include an occasional weasel or stoat, both of which have declined in numbers over much of the country. The ease with which these two little hunters can be shot or trapped may be only partly the reason. Both are very inquisitive. When disturbed they will dive for cover. If one stands quite still the chances are that a sharp little head will lift out of the hole or above the grass, an easy target for a gun. Also, any kind of tunnel is a tempting invitation to such slender bodied animals. A gin set inside a pipe can be a fatal lure, as any gamekeeper knows. This instrument of torture is now illegal in the United Kingdom.

The rabbit, which is the prey of the stoat, is still fairly common. Rabbits were only affected by the virus disease of myxomatosis in the northern parts of Epping Forest. In the fields between Debden and Loughton, the rabbit is often seen and will come out to feed at dawn and dusk. It is scattered throughout the Forest in small colonies, from Epping down to Wanstead Park and Bushwood, but each warren seems to be smaller than formerly. Its numbers have decreased overall, whereas those of the hare have risen, judging from the numerous occasions when its loping shape goes by, even in the Forest depths. Traditionally an animal of open fields and downland, the brown hare seems to be penetrating woodland in many places, perhaps taking over former rabbit country. Normally these two species do not mix.

The commonest and most numerous of the mammals is a small rodent, all ears and eyes, the woodmouse. Nocturnal and nimble, it leaps actively across the Forest floor as it forages in the leaf-litter for animal as well as plant food. Here and there may be found a beech nut or hornbeam fruit with a tiny hole neatly nibbled through. In a hawthorn bush a woodmouse will climb up to take a bite out of a hawberry or two. A deserted bird's nest may become a storehouse of food; another hide-out could be under a tree root. Nightly revels of this attractive little animal are revealed in snow when its bunched footprints may be seen leading in every direction, suddenly disappearing where it has dived below the snow crust for shelter and safety.

In the open glades beneath the coarse tussock grass may be seen the tunnels cut through by the blunt-faced, short-tailed field vole. Its nest of grass and leaves is made above ground, but securely hidden beneath a log or inside a grass hummock. It is a fairly strict vegetarian. Plagues of these voles in olden times devastated some grassy areas, which were said to be suffering from vole-sickness. There is an old record of this condition occurring in Essex. Along the Forest borders, on the banks of ditches and lanes, is the home of the bank vole. It has a more russet-coloured coat, and adds insects to its plant diet.

The tiny harvest mouse is not really a woodland animal; and it has now gone from the fields around the Forest, where it was once reported. Changes in farming practice, and the general absence of corn crops may be the reason. This tiny rodent, which builds a nest around the stalks of cereals, has been driven out of the fields; it stands no chance against the modern reaper.

The charming, furry tailed dormouse, once found along the hedgerows at Chingford, Loughton and Epping, has also probably gone from the district, but the cause is unknown. The hedge-rows still exist, so does the honeysuckle from which it builds its nest; also food is no problem. Pesticides and hedgerow cutting may be to blame, and there is some risk from the uncertain winters that occur these days. Normally the dormouse is in deep winter sleep from November to March. In mild spells, which may now extend into January, it wakes up and perhaps cannot find sufficient food to keep up its energy, and so dies. This delightful creature, which was a common schoolboy's pet in my youth, is seldom seen by today's children.

Squirrels, that is, the native red squirrel, are also no more part of the Forest. The red squirrel managed to survive in the district much longer than anywhere else close to London, partly due to the safety of trees, but also because of introduction. A number of Continental reds, bought in Leadenhall Market, were released at Epping in 1910. All my own sightings of red squirrels have been of this dark variety. The species has a wide distribution through Europe and northern Asia, and is divided into many races. The West European form, which may be almost black in some parts of Germany, is *Sciurus vulgaris vulgaris*. The native British race, seen in Thetford Chase nearest to Epping, is *Sciurus vulgaris leucorus*. It has a tail which bleaches almost white in summer (*leucorus* is Greek for a white tail). It also occurs in parts of Scotland, Wales and the West Country. My last view of a red was in Monk Wood in 1967.

In its place are now plenty of American greys, *Sciurus caroliniensis*. Introduced during the last century, the grey squirrel is known to have escaped from a number of centres, such as Woburn Park and the Regent's Park Zoo. From the zoo it probably spread up the Lea Valley to reach the Forest. The first pair to be seen turned up in Bury Wood near Chingford in 1935. In his report to the London Natural History Society for 1937, F. J. Johnson mentions the campaign which was immediately set up by the conservators to exterminate this invader, urging vigilance on everyone to report any further occurrences. This failed and the greys spread rapidly, even to parks and gardens, no doubt encouraged by well-meaning folk who fed them. This still goes on today in parks, although the government's encouragement to kill these squirrels, by putting a bounty on their tails, has certainly reduced their numbers. The main concern over the greys was the damage they can cause to standing timber grown by forestry. By feeding on the leading shoots, a squirrel can stunt a young tree's growth, and cause it to break into side branches thereby affecting the graining with knots. In Epping Forest, where the trees are grown for amenity only, this is not serious, but the area could act as a reservoir for breeding. I remember seeing anything up to twenty or more grey squirrels during a single day's ramble, before there were organised shoots by the keepers. The real trouble where damage is concerned is not because they are squirrels, but because there are too many of them. In moderate numbers, as with the alien rabbit, they are welcome and attractive additions to our native fauna. Indeed, with their habit of hiding food by burying it, squirrels must have planted many an acorn. Who knows how many Forest oaks started life in this way?

During a Forest walk one may disturb a tiny, restless creature with a long quivering nose. This is the common shrew; about 3in long, it is a quarrelsome mite caught up in an insatiable hunger. This is no rodent, but a tiny and fearless hunter which forages in the leaf-litter, pouncing on any worm, beetle or woodlouse it may happen to meet. It keeps going night and day, winter and summer, burning up energy, and seldom living more than one year. The common shrew is still fairly plentiful, but the pigmy shrew, a mere 2in long, may have gone. This could also be the case with the water shrew, which once lived along the Forest streams and the banks of the two rivers.

Moles turn up occasionally in Forest soil and in bordering fields, also causing annoyance in gardens or sports grounds. Many an old mole-hill in a Forest glade, now covered with turf, has been used as an ants' nest, or a sunning platform for a basking adder or grass snake. In spite of a nightly toll on the highway, the wandering hedgehog still turns up in fair numbers, and is welcomed by understanding gardeners.

Bats are the least known of the mammals, since they are mostly active on the wing, and then only at night. During hibernation, the odd specimen, or even a small colony, may occasionally be found in a hollow tree or behind loose bark. Of the thirteen British species of bat, probably no more than six are Forest dwellers; I am only acquainted with three. The common pipistrelle can be seen flitting through the glades and over bordering gardens on summer evenings, hunting the night-flying midges and gnats. Larger and more purposeful in flight is the noctule. Like the pipistrelle, it haunts woodlands and will hibernate in hollow trees as well as buildings. The bat seen in broad daylight flying over a Forest pond is in all probability the Daubenton's or water bat.

# 9

# BIRDS

One of the more popular branches of natural history is the study of birds, whether by a serious ornithologist or as a pastime by a bird-watcher. Over the years Epping Forest has received its fair share of attention, and records by observers have been published in a number of journals, such as the *London Naturalist,* the *London Bird Report* and the *Essex Naturalist* (see Bibliography). On glancing through the various lists, a certain consistency in the species may be noted. This is not surprising since birds are very much tied to their surroundings, even though they seem to come and go as they please. Each is a specialist, and fits into a certain habitat which supplies it with two of its chief needs—the correct kind of food and the right type of nesting site. This habitat could be a desert, a mountain, the sea-shore, a pond, moorland or a woodland.

Epping Forest, with its bushes and trees, is largely a supporter of woodland birds. The greater spotted woodpecker is an obvious example of a bird built for such surroundings. The tree is its birthplace, home and larder. Its body is accordingly built to a design for clinging to and climbing over bark. The strong beak acts as a chisel for nest-making, digging out hidden food or splitting nuts, and the long tongue winkles out grubs from the cracks and crevices. It proclaims the tree as its domain loudly and in no uncertain terms to rival males, as it drums its challenge from the sounding board of a dead branch. This remarkable sound echoes through the trees of the Forest every springtime.

Actually the true woodland birds are few in number, and occur in those places away from the open where the trees form a closed canopy, as in the depths of Monk Wood. Most Forest birds favour the more open glades, rides and borders where there are thorn bushes and undergrowth. A third group prefer even more open spaces, such as the commons and plains, and a fourth belong to the water.

Among the truly tree birds of the deeper parts of the Forest there are few 'regulars', but one might expect to see the nuthatch, the tree-creeper, the three woodpeckers, and the tawny owl. The wryneck is now so rare, and its future for the whole country so uncertain, that it may never return to the Forest. It was last recorded at Loughton in 1949.

The green woodpecker is the largest of the three woodpeckers and unmistakable. Above, it is a rich dark green, and below more yellow green. Crown and nape are crimson; the male has a crimson moustache, the female a black one. This is the bird which utters the ringing, laughter-like cry, giving it the alternative name of yaffle. It might also be called the ant woodpecker, as it is more likely to be seen on the ground foraging for ants, especially in the glades where there are ants' nests in the old mole hummocks.

The greater spotted woodpecker, or pied woodpecker, has a chequered pattern of black and white. The male has a crimson splash on the back of its head. Of all the woodpeckers, it does most of the drumming. The lesser spotted woodpecker, no bigger than a sparrow, is less easy to discern, as it shyly keeps to the topmost branches. Here the male has a crimson crown. A rounded hole in a tree may be a woodpecker's nest—and a new one, if fresh chippings litter the ground. If any young are inside, they can sometimes be made to call loudly by gently tapping the trunk. Woodpeckers have been known to take over nest-boxes by enlarging the hole. People like myself who live on the Forest borders see the occasional woodpecker visiting the bird table, especially if some fat or nuts are put out.

The tawny owl is still a common Forest resident; it is heard on most nights, giving its quavering call among the silent trees as the sounds of daytime die away. It nests in a hollow tree. By day it may be spotted at its roost, especially if the tree has a covering of ivy. At the foot of the tree may be found the food pellets which the owl coughs up after each meal. These can be broken up in water and examined for traces of the last meal. Fur and feather, bones, teeth, even entire skulls of tiny mammals, occasional birds and such insects as beetles tell their own story. These are the main dwellers of the closed woodlands.

Birds visiting such areas, usually after food, come in from outside, and include the jay and woodpigeon. The jay will betray its whereabouts with a screeching cry like the sound of tearing linen, which can be most aggravating to an observer trying to stalk deer or remain unnoticed. The clatter of a flock of woodpigeons taking flight is even more of a giveaway. The woodpigeon, known also as the ringdove from the white patches on its neck, has few admirers among farmers or gardeners. Even naturalists get annoyed at times when they dominate the bird table. This bird has invaded the towns and can be seen in plenty in the Inner London parks. Oddly enough, there it has no fear of man, but to approach a pigeon in the Forest would take great patience and skill.

Shooting the woodpigeon and the jay has been a policy of the conservators over the years, and is a regular practice among gamekeepers on private estates and woods around the Forest. In the 1880s, protest meetings were held by the Essex Field Club deploring these activities, and Buxton led an appeal to neighbouring landowners to protect certain birds, such as the tawny owl, magpie, lapwing, heron, kingfisher, and all hawks except the sparrow-hawk. Today these and most other birds are protected. The dashing flight of the sparrow-hawk through the Forest trees is seldom seen these days. It is now generally agreed that the birds of prey have suffered very severely from the use of weed-killers and insecticides (see page 180). The killing of jays was very much regretted by the earlier Forest naturalists. Today there are mixed feelings about its control. It does raid the occasional nest, yet it is a handsome bird. The same might be said of the magpie, which has increased of late and now appears in gardens as far south as Wanstead. A close view will reveal a beautiful iridescent sheen on its dark feathers.

Members of the tit family are usually heard before they are seen. These little acrobats, commonly seen in the garden, search the branches and leaves for insects in summer, and seeds in winter. The wheezy call of the little blue-tit and the monotonous 'teacher-teacher' of the great-tit are familiar sounds. During the winter days they quarter the woods in small parties, and one is suddenly aware of their presence as they pass through the trees. For a moment or two one is surrounded by tiny, flitting shapes calling to each other, then they pass on and the trees are empty and silent once more.

On the ground, foraging in the leaf-litter for seeds and other food morsels, a flock of finches may be disturbed. If they are chaffinches, which are common enough, it could be that they are mostly males. There is a tendency to segregate during winter, so that the cock birds form 'bachelor parties', living up to part of their scientific name—*coelebs*, meaning just that. The resident chaffinch is often joined in winter by a visitor from the north, the brambling, which has a fondness for beech-mast. The mottled, blackish head and red shoulder patches in both sexes distinguish it from the chaffinch. Also in winter comes the siskin, a neat little bird of yellow-green appearance, with a black head and chin, and a strongly forked tail. It has a fondness for alder trees which grow near water, and can usually be seen by the lakesides in Wanstead and Higham's parks. Another finch is the lesser red-poll, resembling a miniature linnet, but with a black chin instead of reddish breast. Underneath it is white, and the crown of the head a glossy crimson. It haunts the birch thickets, feeding on the innumerable seeds, and can often be heard twittering in the tree tops around High Beech. A useful guide in looking for this winter trio would be: brambling—beech, siskin—alder, and redpoll—birch.

An occasional winter resident which uses the Forest more for shelter, and is rarely noticed unless disturbed, is the woodcock.

Few ground-nesting birds are more remarkably camouflaged in what is called 'dead leaf' pattern than this game bird. I have seen it fly off from some damp hollow in wintertime, from places as far apart as the Lower Forest and Wanstead Park. During my camping days by the Forest border near Debden, between Theydon Bois and Loughton, a woodcock would appear at the same evening hour, flying exactly the same course past our camp site, uttering a peculiar groaning sound. This is the flight of the cock bird, known as 'roding'.

A rare winter visitor to the Forest is a long-distance traveller which, in ornithological terms, has 'irrupted' from its native home in northern Europe, due to severe weather conditions. This is the waxwing, so named because of the yellow and red colours on its plumage, resembling drops of sealing wax. With its head crest, this finch is unmistakable, and its appearance is a red-letter day for any bird-watcher. I have had the pleasure of seeing it only once, during the severe 1946–7 winter, which was called a 'waxwing year'.

Turning to the summer visitors, towards late March or early April the keen bird student awaits the first appearance of those little travellers from Africa, the warblers. There are three leaf-warblers in particular, looking very similar but each with its distinctive song: the chiff-chaff, willow-warbler and wood-warbler. They usually arrive in that order, quietly entering the Forest, even pausing a day or two in one's garden. They search for insects among the spreading tree-leaves, but nest discreetly in heavy undergrowth along the Forest fringe. Close to the ground, bound to a patch of tall grass, or low in a bush, may be found a soft, deep nest with an opening to one side. Leaf-warblers always construct a domed nest.

It is in the glades, along the rides and where the open spaces are scattered with thorn and bramble, that the majority of the Forest birds may be seen and heard. They share the hawthorn, sloe, blackberry and rose thickets with these warblers, and include the more familiar thrush, blackbird, robin, finch and wren. An interesting bird to watch is the spotted flycatcher. Perched on a projecting branch, it suddenly flies into the air to catch a passing insect, then returns to its perch. On a quiet summer's day, if close enough, one can hear the snap of its beak as each insect is caught. Equally characteristic is the song-flight of the tree-pipit. From a high perch it flies straight upwards in song, then seems to collapse and sail downwards, ending its song in a series of tired notes like an unwound clock. It nests on the ground in spite of its name, and is a victim of the parasitic cuckoo. Of late years the cuckoo has decreased considerably throughout the land, and its familiar call can no longer be termed a nuisance. In my camping days I can remember being awakened at dawn by the incessant call which went on all day. More to our liking was the serenade of that poet's darling, the nightingale. Happily, this is still a common summer visitor to the Forest. It can be heard, even seen with careful approach, by visiting one of the many thickets where there are crowded thorn bushes. Two such good spots are behind the Connaught Water and along Fairmead Bottom. Here, during May and the first half of June, this splendid songster may be heard the night through, and even at all daylight hours, competing with the noise of nearby traffic. On one occasion I took two bird-loving American friends to hear our star performer. They stood with me for an hour on Chingford Plain, entranced with the melody of five birds. Later they wrote to tell me that their tape recording had proved a great hit with the members of their Audubon Society back home.

A 'speciality' of the Forest, if it may so be called, is the redstart, recognised by the way in which it flirts its reddish brown tail when perched on a branch. Its fondness for holes in which to nest has attracted it to the old pollarded hornbeams which are full of suitable nest sites. In neighbouring gardens it may also choose a gap in a wall where a brick is missing. A red-letter day for any ornithologist in Britain would be the sight of a thrush-like bird coloured a vivid golden yellow—the golden oriole. This summer visitor to southern England turns up all too infrequently, usually in wooded areas, and was last reported near High Beech in 1942.

Two other rare summer birds, are the red-backed shrike and the nightjar. This shrike was a regular nester among the thorn bushes of Fairmead Bottom, where I once found its 'larder' of insects, a shrew and a young bird, all dead and impaled on the thorns near the nest. From this practice it has been named the butcher-bird. About jay size, it has a fierce expression and strong, hooked beak. Twelve pairs bred in 1945 and it is worth looking out for, if passing that way, as it may still return. The same goes for the strange, nocturnal fern-owl, as the nightjar is sometimes called. A bird of heathland and difficult to see, its presence is revealed by the curious churring sound which goes on for minutes on end through the dusk. It nests on the ground among the bracken and heather, and is perfectly camouflaged. Up till 1952 it nested regularly.

The more open spaces, such as Wanstead and Leyton Flats, also Chingford Plain to the north, may harbour a number of species of birdlife which tend to avoid wooded areas. The skylark still sings its melody from the blue skies, and may nest in the more undisturbed grassy patches. It is the woodlark that one should keep a watchful eye for. It seems to have returned to the Forest—1946 being the first record by the London Natural History Society since 1905. Smaller than the skylark, but of similar colour, it has a shorter tail and fuller head crest. Its song is even sweeter than that of its cousin, and the flight not so high. It usually circles about 50ft up, then planes down to the ground.

A bird once so popular with the London cockney, and caught in thousands by the old bird-catchers, is the linnet. The brownish plumage is enhanced in the summer dress of the cock, with a crimson crown and forehead. An occasional small flock may be spotted on Chingford Plain or Wanstead Flats during wintertime, keeping up an incessant twittering. Gorse bushes are an attraction as nest sites, and where these occur, as at Wanstead, one may also be lucky in seeing the handsome stonechat, making its odd-sounding call like two pebbles knocked together. Down from the north in severe winter weather comes the hooded crow, and on rare occasions the great grey shrike. Much more regular as winter visitors are the two Scandinavian thrushes, the red-wing and fieldfare. The redwing is perhaps more a woodland bird to be expected in gardens. It has reddish patches under each wing. The fieldfares keep in flocks, and will quarter the hedgerows and places where the thorn bushes provide them with berries to eat.

When these birds have left us for their journey back home to the north, the earliest of the summer visitors arrives, in March. This is the wheatear, easily recognised by its sandy grey colouring, black wings, and black and white tail which bobs up and down in redstart fashion. It is a passage migrant through the Forest, on its way to the hillsides of the Pennines and Wales where it nests among stones and walls. Shortly after World War II had ended, some anti-aircraft gunpits on Wanstead Flats remained deserted for three years. Each year, in March and on the return journey in late September, wheatears paused to rest on their travels, using the gun-pits as a kind of 'staging post'.

The few large ponds and lakes in and around the Forest attract and add to the bird population. Apart from the usual residents, such as moorhen, coot, mallard and mute swan, a surprisingly high number of water birds and marsh dwellers turn up, either in spring for breeding purposes or as winter visitors. Some waters to watch are the two lakes, in Higham's and Wanstead parks, the Connaught Water, the Eagle Pond at Snaresbrook, and the Basin on the Wanstead Golf Links. From a bedroom window facing the Basin I can watch the courtship of the great crested grebe, and in early morning see a lonely heron standing like a sentinel at its fishing post, while the heavy commuter traffic goes by on its way to town. Canada geese pay fleeting visits, but do not usually stay, although they nested in Wanstead Park in 1970. A memorable day in January 1969 saw the brief appearance of the fish-hunting merganser.

An interesting record of counts of the heron has been kept by the London Natural History Society. This was originally started by the Essex Field Club, and clearly shows the gradual decline of the famous heronry of Wanstead Park. The Borough of Wanstead and Woodford had a heron on its civic crest, formerly that of the lord of Wanstead manor, Sir John Heron. This bird was also chosen as the badge still worn on the caps and blazers of the students of my old high school. In those days of the 1920s and 1930s, herons were a common sight wheeling over Wanstead Park or standing in the water. Today, alas, they no longer nest there, and only occasionally does a heron pass by. Disturbance by the rooks, or perhaps water pollution and a shortage of fish, may have been the cause of their decline. Happily, the herons have not deserted the district, and can now be seen on the island of one of the reservoirs in the Lea Valley. The severe winter of 1962–3 did much harm to water birds, and nearly wiped out the gaudy kingfisher. I saw it frequently as a boy, both in Wanstead Park and along the Roding. Whilst fishing in the Perch Pond one morning, I watched a kingfisher diving for its meal from one of the rowing boats. Having caught one fish it then flew across and settled on the tip of my rod!

The variety of scenery which provides different habitats has undoubtedly a lot to do with the rich bird life of the Forest. The nest sites are there, so is the food, also much freedom from disturbance. Some species are now rare if not extinct, whereas others have actually increased. With the spread of houses pressing in on the Forest, more gardens have come into being which have undoubtedly helped to build up the bird population—in other words, the very birds which normally live in woodlands. At one time such birds were trapped in large numbers for food or as cage birds; also, there were more hawks about. Today, with the scarcity of birds of prey, an increased affection for and desire to protect wild birds, and a waning of egg-collecting, the situation is quite different. Despite outside pressures, much is now in the birds' favour and, so long as their habitats and nest-sites remain secure, those of us who love the Forest and its wildlife should be able to enjoy the company and song of its birds for many years to come.

# 10

# INSECTS

Oh, what is this that shines so bright
  And in the lonely place
Hangs out his small green lamp at night,
  The dewy bank to grace!
It is a glow-worm, still and pale
  It shines the whole night long.
                    the Rev William Lisle Bowles,
                          Canon of St Paul's

One of the most concentrated areas of insect life in Britain is in
the woodland habitat. Almost every plant, and every part of it,
from leaf to wood, fruit and root, has its insect attendant. Even
the litter of the Forest floor is occupied; so is the fallen log, the
toadstool, each dead animal and its dung. Only a brief summary
of the Forest insects can be given here, mostly those which I have
encountered in the past thirty years or so, while making serious
studies and taking records.

In the past Epping Forest has had its fair share of entomologists who have come to collect and observe its insect life. Most
of this work, however, dates back to earlier years when enthu-
siastic amateurs were more active in this field. Today there is
some need for more investigation into these old records, since so
much has altered of late in our countryside. I have noticed a
distinct change in the frequency of certain species in the Forest
area. Some have decreased, even disappeared, while others have
increased. Reasons for this are complex and not fully under-
stood, but certain factors have taken toll of the insect population.
The pesticide war waged by the farmer and gardener must have

caused huge casualties among insects. We may be glad to do with fewer aphids, gnats and house-flies, but in attacking these we are also killing off the useful bee and attractive butterfly.

Since the Forest is spared the use of chemicals, it might be argued that insecticides do not enter into this problem. Even so, careless spraying does carry on the wind, as I have witnessed a few times. Another hazard could be the song birds, whose numbers are no longer kept in check by birds of prey. In either case we have an upset in the food chain. Even so there is still much insect life to be seen in the Forest. All of those noted here I have seen myself. The most obvious are among the fly family, or Diptera. Of these two-winged insects everyone should know the familiar crane-fly, or daddy-longlegs, *Tipula oleracea*. It breeds in grass to produce grubs called leatherjackets. Vast swarms of adults may suddenly appear in a field, sometimes a garden, bordering the Forest, also in a grassy Forest glade. A large fly resembling a bee both in shape and markings, even making a bee-like buzzing sound, commonly turns up under the trees during hot summers. This is the gad-fly, *Tabanus bovinus*, which can give a nasty bite and is troublesome to cattle. Also an attacker of animals, especially horses, is the bot-fly, *Gasterophilus equi*. It is also bee-like in appearance, a rich, chestnut brown, and haunts stables. The larva hatches from an egg laid on the horse, and grows in its stomach. It is probably well known to the Forest horse-riders. Out in the woods occurs the troublesome horse fly, *Hippobosca equina*. It clings tightly to the tormented animal with its strong claws. Another large, bee-like fly, seen hovering in the air like a helicopter but also capable of darting suddenly in any direction, is the drone fly, *Eristalis tenax*. It is usually seen in numbers during late summer, sitting on the Michaelmas daisies. Its curious grub, called the rat-tailed maggot, lives in unsavoury places such as drains, muddy pools and ditches, and has a long and extensible 'tail'. This is actually a breathing tube which can reach up to the surface as much as a foot long, in order to take in fresh air. Hovering over the patches of horse dung in the Forest rides, or around cow pats in the fields, can be seen the orange coloured dung fly, *Scatophaga stercoraria*. Apart from these large and conspicuous flies there are innumerable small species broadly described as midges and gnats, some of which bite. A person's allergy to bites varies. Some people hardly notice them, while others may feel quite ill after a dose of bites during a Forest ramble.

The beetles, or Coleoptera, make an interesting study into Forest life, and show how adaptable these creatures are to the different food niches. Some are real hunters, swift in movement, ready to pounce upon some other insect or grub. Of these, the handsome tiger beetle, *Cicindela campestris*, may turn up in some dry and sandy locality on any one of the open glades. It has a metallic blue body covered by bright green wing-cases. Usually hidden by day under a log or stone lurks the violet ground beetle, *Carabus violaceus*. It also hunts, but will rapidly make for cover if exposed. The devil's coach-horse, *Ocypus olens*, is a fearsome-looking beetle which raises its hind quarters in a threatening manner when disturbed. It is quite harmless, merely giving off an unpleasant smell; the Latin *olens* means 'stinking'. No less an assiduous hunter, but at a very slow pace, is the fascinating glow-worm, *Lampyris noctiluca*. This is the female of a beetle species which is grub-like in build and capable of giving out a light. *Noctiluca*, the Latin for 'little night light', is an excellent name for the tiny glow in the bushes, with which she attracts a mate. He can fly actively, but she moves slowly in pursuit of her favourite prey, a snail. Sometimes even this slow-coach can escape! Glow-worms are patchy in distribution, and usually confined to certain stretches of hedgerow or corners of copses in and around the Forest. In my camping days we used to collect specimens, and keep them in jam-jars hung up in our tents after dark. The pale green light was strong enough to read by.

Ladybirds, also little hunters, are welcomed by gardeners as they help in the war on aphids. Of the forty or so British species, the seven-spot ladybird, *Coccinella septempunctata* is one of the commonest. Apart from entering our homes these useful beetles will sometimes hibernate in the oddest places. I have many times found them tucked away in empty beech-nut cases still attached to the trees. Some beetles act as scavengers. One of these is the dor beetle, *Geotropus stercorarius*, a large, black, rounded, clumsy creature which crawls around like a miniature tank. It is attracted to manure heaps and animal droppings. In the Forest I have found it at the entrance to rabbit burrows, fox earths, and in badgers' latrine pits. Remains of this and other beetles can be found in the droppings of both hedgehog and badger, also toads, since all three will eat beetles.

One very interesting family of beetles are those which bury their food. By undermining a carcass, the body of a dead mouse or bird is entirely covered with earth. This is the work of the burying beetle, *Necrophorus vespillo*, easy to identify because of its dark wing-cases marked with a broad band of orange. By keeping a few of these beetles in a box of earth, in which a dead animal has been placed, the whole mining operation can be watched.

Turning from the ground level to bushes and trees, here also beetles may be found. The bark or engraver beetles, family Scolytidae, occur mainly under the bark of conifers, but also in the old Forest oaks. Holes bored through the bark will show where the adults have emerged after the fashion of the unwelcome furniture beetles in our homes. If the tree is dying, and the bark can be removed, some attractive and often intricate patterns will be seen on the bared wood. These are the tunnels made by the grubs, or wood 'worms', which are a favourite food of woodpeckers. Beetles with long antennae, called longhorns, have larvae which actually penetrate the wood of trees, making tunnels after the fashion of wood-worms. In fact, some furniture beetles live wild in trees. It is said that damage to woodwork is more prevalent in districts where there are wooded areas, such as Epping Forest, and this seems to be borne out by statistics. The common species of furniture beetle is *Anobium striatum*. The adult emerges in June and July, and infested areas should be treated a little before this happens, so as to arrest further egg-laying.

Page 122 (*above*) Young female glow-worm attacking a snail; (*below*) red admiral butterfly, often seen in gardens

On a more widespread scale is damage caused by the death-watch beetle, *Xestobium rufovillosum*. This has been found living naturally in decaying oak and beech trees in the Forest. In buildings it is chiefly associated with oak beams, whether inside cottages or in large mansions. The old oak beams of the Hunting Lodge at Chingford have suffered from this beetle in the past. The tapping noises made by these beetles inside their tunnels, said to be a means of communication, can only be heard in very quiet surroundings. Presumably at a time of grief, when someone was dying, the subdued atmosphere inside the home would make it possible to hear the tapping sound—hence its name 'death-watch'. Among the more impressive wood beetles are the family Lucanidae, or stag beetles. I have found the grubs of two species in the stumps of rotting logs and trees in the Forest. One of these, *Dorcus parallelopipedus*, is about an inch long, and the male has small antler-like mandibles. The second species, *Lucanus cervus*, up to 3in long, is one of our largest beetles. The adult male has prominent 'antlers' and a fearsome aspect, yet it is a gentle creature. I have kept a specimen or two in a box of rotten wood, and fed them on sugar. I once placed some grubs, found in a rotten tree stump, in holes bored in a log in my wild garden. At a later date stag beetles were reported in the neighbourhood, one of these entering a bedroom to the consternation of the occupants.

Members of the beetle family called the Curculionidae can usually be recognised by their elongated heads which form a kind of snout. These are the weevils or 'snout-bearers', which feed on plants. Those which do the most damage to trees by feeding on the leaves are called leaf-rollers. A leaf of, say, oak or beech, is cut through to the midrib by the grub, then rolled up to form a kind of shelter. In the Forest can be found the species *Rhynchites betuleti* on birch, and *Apoderus coryli* on oak or hazel. Those weevils whose larvae tunnel through the leaves are called leaf-miners. Very common on beech is *Orchestes fagi*. Still other weevils feed on nuts, and a species called *Balaninus nucum* may be found inside hazel nuts and acorns. It is interesting how a

H 123

squirrel knows this, and will immediately discard a damaged acorn after a quick sniff.

Everyone must know the maybug or cockchafer, *Melonontha vulgaris*, on sight. Its droning flight is familiar on warm May and June evenings in the Forest area. The grubs which live in the soil and attack the roots of young trees can sometimes become harmful to forestry. Whereas the adult of this species is a rich blue-black with yellow-brown wing-cases, the less common rosechafer or June bug, *Cetonia aurata*, is an attractive copper colour with metallic green wing-covers.

Turning next to the Hymenoptera, the common wasp, *Vespa vulgaris*, still turns up in large numbers, especially during a good summer, and is a familiar invader of the jampot or garden fruit. Generally considered a nuisance, it is seldom regarded as a friend. Yet it is quite inoffensive unless molested, and must do considerable good by attacking other insects which may harm our plants. I have often seen the hunting workers hawking up and down a garden wall or Forest glade where various flies have gathered, and pouncing on their prey after the fashion of dragon-flies. Far less common and even more inoffensive is the larger hornet, *Vespa crabro*. It has a more reddish brown colouring and builds a suspended nest from a tree branch. I remember seeing one in Knighton Woods near the lake when this was still a private estate belonging to the Buxton family.

Much concern has been shown of late over the heavy loss of the hive bee, *Apis mellifera*, largely due to the poison sprays used in gardens. Even so these honey-makers are holding their own, and may occasionally revert to the wild at swarming time. A queen may lead the colony into the Forest, and settle inside a hollow tree. I have come across such hives a number of times. On the other hand, the home of the large wood-ant, *Formica rufa*, has only turned up once, when I found it alongside the Green Ride by Fairmead. Earlier naturalists speak of nests made out of twigs and leaves under the hawthorn bushes. It is perhaps more usual to find this ant among conifers, which are rare in the Forest. Various bumble bees may be encountered during a summer day's ramble, and are a common sight in gardens. Of these the largest, *Bombus terrestris*, has a covering of silky black hair crossed by two conspicuous yellow bands. Its nest is at the end of a long tunnel built into the soil. From here the females will emerge after hibernation. Places to look are in the drier parts of the Forest on the sandy or gravel soils.

The large and handsome wood wasp, *Sirex gigas*, is a stranger to the Forest, since it prefers conifer trees in which to lay its eggs. The harmless 'sting' is really an ovipositor for boring holes through the bark. The grub which hatches out can do much harm to the timber, provided that it avoids the attention of the parasitic ichneumon fly, *Rhyssa persuasoria*. This ingenious creature searches over the bark, and in some manner detects the presence of a wood-wasp grub. Boring down after it the ichneumon lays her egg, so that a rich meal awaits the grub when it hatches. The only time I witnessed this feat was on some alder trees alongside the river Roding, near the old red bridge by Wanstead Park. In this instance it was the smaller and more blue-grey coloured alder woodwasp laying her eggs. Since it also lays eggs on willow, this wasp is much more likely to be seen in the Forest.

# 11

# BUTTERFLIES AND MOTHS

The Emperor Moth, *Saturnia pavonia*: 'What is called Symbol-
ling, or, the coming together, is particularly observable in this
Species. Take a female . . . and set her down in a Box covered
with Gauze; and if within a Mile down the wind there should be
a Male, he presently snuffs the Effluvia exhal'd from her, and
finds her out by the Scent . . .
>               JAMES DITCHFIELD. *A New and Complete Natural
>               History of English Moths and Butterflies* (1749)

In the *London Naturalist* for 1945 a list is given of some fifty-six
species of butterflies for the society's area—within a radius of
twenty miles from St Paul's. This covers the Forest, for which
forty of this total were listed, both recent and extinct. Twenty-
one species were then still to be found. Today it is very doubtful
whether more than a dozen can be seen, even during a good
summer season. Of these, some of the 'whites' and 'browns', the
Vanessids and 'blues' are still fairly common.

The large or cabbage white, *Pieris brassicae*, still turns up in
heavy numbers during some yearly migrations, for many travel
over from the Continent and may wander into the Forest. Less
frequent is the small white, *P. rapae*. An attack by the caterpillar
of the former will turn a cabbage into a ragged skeleton, whereas
the smaller species tends to bore holes through the leaves to reach
the heart. The pretty little orange-tip, *Euchloe cardamine*, is confined more to the bordering lanes and to the valleys of the Lea
and Roding where the two food plants grow. The caterpillars
feed on the cuckoo flower and hedge parsley. The attractive
brimstone, *Gonepteryx rhamni*, is now somewhat a rare occur-

rence, and has not been seen much of late. Lack of its food plant may be the reason. The caterpillar feeds on the leaves of buckthorn. It was once called the butter-coloured fly, and has given its name to the whole group. The clouded yellow, *Colias croceus*, is a summer migrant which now and then crosses the Channel in large numbers, reaching well inland. It may be seen visiting garden flowers, and in fields bordering the Forest. Should it lay eggs, then the caterpillars may be found on lucerne and clover. It is doubtful whether this species can survive our winters.

Of the handsome and conspicuous vanessid butterflies some are quite common in and around the Forest. Their caterpillars feed on nettle, and the adults are attracted to garden flowers and fallen fruit. The buddleia, or butterfly bush, is often grown in gardens for its scent and to attract the adults. Some of these will hibernate, and are usually the first to be seen in the following spring. Two of these are the peacock, *Nymphalis io*, and the small tortoiseshell, *Aglais urticae*. Both have nettle-feeding caterpillars, and may be found in winter sleep inside the garden shed, or in a hollow Forest tree. I once found a peacock butterfly in an old pollard which it shared with a bat. The red admiral, *Vanessa atalanta*, was once called the red admirable butterfly, a name which it fully deserves. This is mainly a migrant, but may occasionally get through an English winter. More sporadic in its visits is the painted lady, *Vanessa cardui*. The comma, *Polygonia c-album*, is named after the small white 'comma mark' under each hind wing. It is reported as being on the increase throughout the country. Perhaps more people are recognising it as distinct from the tortoiseshell which it resembles. Only once have I seen a white admiral, *Limenites camilla*, a well-known butterfly of the New Forest, but now seldom seen close to London.

Of the more sombre coloured 'browns', the meadow brown, *Maniola jurtina*, is the commonest Forest resident, to be seen in most of the glades and grassy places. Also fairly frequent is the small heath, *Coenonympha pamphilus*. The 'blues' seem to have disappeared of late years, except for the common blue, *Polyommatus icarus*, which chooses a number of food plants, such as plantain and clover. There is also an occasional holly blue, *Celastrina argiolus*.

Gone are the days when three of the most handsome species, now rare for most of Britain, dwelt in and around the Forest. The purple emperor, *Apatura iris*, used to be seen flying around the old oaks in Doubleday's time. Also, the migrant Camberwell beauty, named after its first discovery in the little country village of Camberwell, turned up in some past years, and would hibernate inside the old pollards. To see either of these today would thrill the modern Forest naturalist, as indeed would the sight of the swallow-tail, *Papilio machaon*, surely our loveliest butterfly. It used to inhabit the marshy places along the river valleys, especially the Lea, and was probably known to Izaak Walton in his time. Today it is confined to the fenland of Norfolk.

Moths are far more numerous than butterflies, both in species and numbers, though much less noticeable except when they enter a lighted room. Yet, somehow the frequency with which they entered my bedroom when a boy, and the many we found clinging to old walls, wooden fences and forest trees seems a thing of the past. No doubt the brilliance of the modern mercury vapour trap would bring in a tidy haul, but its use inside the Forest is contrary to the bye-laws, as indeed is the old method of sugaring. Since the Forest has been overcollected in the past, further mass captures are to be discouraged. A number of moths are associated with woodlands since their caterpillars feed on the bushes and trees. Of these there are two whose larvae actually live inside the wood. One is the goat moth, *Cossus ligniperda*. The large female has a wingspan almost 3¾in across. Its handsome reddish-brown caterpillar tunnels into the solid wood of elm and willow trunks for three years before the adult emerges. I once saw the damage caused to an old apple tree after it was felled. The disagreeable smell which comes from the damaged wood has given this moth its name. The chrysalis forms in the ground, inside a cocoon of silk and wood chippings. The smaller leopard moth, *Zeuzera pyrina*, about 3in across, has pale wings speckled in black. The caterpillars seem to occur more in the branches rather than the main trunk, and will turn up in a number of broad-leaved trees. It is also in the Forest records, although I have never found it. These two are usually found by chance.

Much more conspicuous, and far smaller, are the so-called 'defoliators' whose caterpillars devour the leaves of Forest trees. Certain small moths are responsible, such as the oak-leaf roller moth, *Tortrix viridana*. This pretty little moth with apple green wings may be seen in July fluttering around the oak trees. If a branch is shaken a small cloud of these moths may be put to flight, soon to settle again. The females lay their eggs on the leaves. These hatch the following spring. When fully fed a caterpillar will roll up the edge of a leaf binding it with silk, and pupate inside. The winter moth, *Cheimatobia brumata*, and the mottled umber, *Hybernia defoliaria*, have caterpillars which hump their bodies as they move, and are called 'loopers'. These attack oak and beech leaves. In both cases the female is wingless. They hatch in October or November from a pupa buried in the soil, to which the caterpillar has descended the previous summer by means of a silken thread. Crawling up the trunk the female meets a winged male, mates, then lays eggs in the bark crevices. Caterpillars appear next spring and are fully grown by June when they descend to pupate. In some summers I have seen entire oak, beech and hornbeam trees stripped of their leaves, the bared branches festooned with fine curtains of silk. These are probably what visitors walk against during a summer ramble under the trees. As I walked beneath the trees it was difficult to avoid the dangling caterpillars. Woodland birds, such as tits and leaf-warblers, must eat these caterpillars in prodigious numbers, and help in their control. The same could be said of the parasitic ichneumon flies which lay their eggs inside these caterpillars so that they become weakened, and are easy prey to the birds. Ironically, the ichneumons are also eaten in the process, so that one wonders where the ultimate control of these caterpillars lies. Certainly of recent years these caterpillar 'plagues' are far milder than they used to be.

The large family of Noctuid moths are mostly of dull colouring when at rest, blending perfectly with the bark, fence or wall on which they happen to settle. W. Cole, in Buxton's *Epping Forest*, related an interesting story of a rare noctuid, *Erastria venustula*, found nowhere else in Britain and discovered by Doubleday in the Forest just once, in 1845. Much later, at the turn of the century, it began turning up regularly in Monk Wood. I have searched but never found it. Large and handsome, with a 3¼in span of ochre-coloured wings, is the oak-eggar, *Lasiocampa quercus*, so-called from the shape of its cocoon. Its caterpillar feeds on hawthorn, sloe and oak, all common in the Forest. I have sometimes found the brownish caterpillar with its shiny black rings and white stripes along the sides. This is one of the moths noted for its powerful attraction by the female, which is called the 'assembly'. Males are drawn to her from far and wide as she lurks in the bushes. A female carried in a box on a walk through oak-eggar country will bring in the males from all directions, so powerful is the scent.

The vapourer moth, *Orgyia antiqua*, is common enough around London, and has even been recorded in some of the inner parks. It lays its eggs on numerous species of trees and shrubs, so may turn up in the Forest. Where the Forest willows and poplars grow may be found the furry, silver-grey puss moth, *Dicranura vinula*. As a boy I knew it well in Wanstead Park and along the Roding. I remember how we used to touch the caterpillar gently, to make it push out its two purplish whips from the end of its body.

Hawk moths frequently appear in the Forest area, and are mostly detected by their handsome caterpillars with the curious 'tail' at the end of the body. The adults are on the wing on warm summer nights, seeking out scented flowers such as tobacco plant and honeysuckle, in gardens and the Forest. Some moths are named after the food plant of the caterpillar, such as the privet, poplar and lime hawk moths. The rose-green coloured elephant hawk, *Choerocampa elpenor*, lays on the willow herb, which grows in many parts of the Forest, and the handsome eyed-hawk, *Smerinthus ocellatus*, searches out sallow and willow.

It is to be hoped that these butterflies and moths will grace the glades and rides as part of the Forest scene so long as the trees remain standing.

# FLOWERS OF THE FOREST

A flower lover, familiar with the carpets of primroses, bluebells, anemones and foxgloves which he has found in other woodlands, may express disappointment when visiting Epping Forest. For a large part, even in springtime when many woodland plants are in bloom, he will find an endless carpet of dead leaves under a rather gloomy atmosphere of silent trees. Mosses and bracken, with here and there clumps of holly, are common enough, and in late summer the fungi fruit in abundance, but where are the flowers?

It is only by making a comparison of various lists of flowers which have been recorded in the past that one can get some idea of the changing flora of this ancient woodland. Since Richard Warner's day (see page 160) many species have disappeared, whereas, oddly enough, others which one might have expected to have died out still survive. Apart from Warner's *Plantae Woodfordiensis* of 1771, there are further lists to be consulted, notably those of the Forster brothers, who collected in the area (see pages 161–2), and Buxton in his *Epping Forest*. However, the first serious attempt at assessing the position of the Forest flowers was made by R. W. Robbins in 1915 (Transactions of the London Natural History Society). In this communication he quotes Buxton's list of 436 species, of which seventy-six were unknown to him. On the other hand he added twenty-five extra species, giving a balance of 385. This may seem a reasonably high number, yet Robbins challenges the statement made by Buxton that 'the Forest is for its extent particularly rich in its flora'.

An approximate 30 per cent of all possible species occurred in the Forest during Robbins' day. He gives an extensive list of his findings, some of which have almost certainly disappeared. These include the grass of parnassus, herb paris, whortleberry, and bird's-nest orchid, to mention one or two. On the other hand, there are some unusual survivors which are very localised over southern England, yet still to be seen in the Forest. Examples are the bog-bean, water violet, butcher's broom, bladderwort and flowering rush. The reasons for the scarcity of the commonplace bluebell, primrose, anemone and foxglove are discussed by Robbins. He suggests that these showy plants have suffered at the hands of vandals, in particular those commercially minded collectors intent on selling their ill-gotten gains. This is almost certainly the case with the ferns, such as the common polypody which once grew extensively in the crowns of the old pollards, but today is almost extinct. At one time such plants ended up in the Victorian conservatories when the 'fernery' was a popular feature.

The primrose might always have been somewhat uncommon, since it prefers the damper woodlands, and much of the Forest on the higher ground and valley slopes is of a dry nature. Isolated plants can still be found in the wetter Lower Forest beyond Epping. The scarcity of bluebells, heavily gathered by visitors at one time, may also be due in part to foraging badgers. Also, where there is constant pressure on the soil from pedestrians and horses, the bulbs die off. The odd specimens seen are usually out of harm's way, growing under the shelter of bushes. One of the finest shows of bluebells today is in Wanstead Park, now part of the Forest. Those growing on the islands of the ornamental waters make an attractive blue haze mirrored in the water. Foxgloves and anemones are also a rare sight on actual Forest soil unless one knows of a quiet and hidden spot. I have seen both, in the Lower Forest to the north, and in Wanstead Park to the south.

As far back as 1892 the *Essex Naturalist* reported that 'the primrose and foxglove are now seldom seen in bloom'. These two, also the bluebell, are mentioned in Warner's *Plantae* as being quite common:

> HYACINTHUS (non-scriptus) English Hyacinth or Harebells. In woods and under hedges: common. Found in Mr Warner's large field in plenty.
> DIGITALIS (purpurea). Purple Foxglove. By the roadside, under hedges, near old gravel pits, and in the shady parts of the Forest: common. It is sometimes found with a white flower but very uncommon.
> PRIMULA (vulgaris). Common Primrose. In woods, on the sides of fields and under hedges: very common.

It might be of interest to add that Warner also recorded two other primulas, the cowslip and the false oxlip which today have almost certainly gone from the Forest. He gave them both under the same specific name:

> PRIMULA (veris). Common Pagils, or Cowslips. In meadows: very common.
> PRIMULA (veris). Great Cowslips or Oxlips. In woods, under hedges and in meadows. Found in a meadow, near Wray House, Sir James Wright's, adjoining the river Rhodon: uncommon.

Of these two the cowslip is usually associated with chalky ground, as on the downlands, and occurs commonly in North Essex. Here also is to be found the true oxlip, *Primula elatior*. Much study has gone into these three primulas and their hybrids, but little attention seems to have been given to their demands of soil conditions. From what is known of the present whereabouts and habitat conditions of these attractive plants, it would appear that the oxlip, not the primrose, should do very well if introduced into the Forest, provided that people would leave it alone.

Warner does not mention the wood anemone, *Anemone nemorosa*, which is found in fair numbers on the slopes of Upshire overlooking the Lea Valley along the edge of the Forest. Long before Warner recorded his Forest list, the herbs of the woods and wayside were being gathered and identified by medical men known as herbalists. One of these was William Turner. In the second part of his famous *Herbal*, published in 1562 in Cologne during his exile, there appears the first scientific record of Essex plants, only four species. They are the butcher's broom, *Ruscus aculeatus*, a species of lime, *Tilia*, a hellebore, probably *Helleborus viridis*, and the mistletoe, *Viscum album*. Two are worth mentioning. The little butcher's broom still found in the Forest is the very first scientifically recorded Essex plant. This is what Turner wrote:

> Ruscus is named in Greke myrsine agria, that is myrtus sylvestris, in Barbarus latin bruscus, in English Kneholme, or Knehull, and of other Butcher broume, and of sour Petigre. I never sawe it in Germany, therefore I know not the Dutche name for it. Ruscus called of Dioscorides Myrtus sylvestris hath a leafe lyke unto a myrtell tree, but broder lyke in fashon unto a lance, sharp in the top. It hath a rounde fruyte in the middes of the lefe, rede when it is ripe with a harde Kirnel within. The twigges are bowing lyke vinde braunches, which come out of the route, they are tough a cubit high, full of leaves, the routes are lyke unto grasse binding, tarte in taste and something bitter. This bushe groweth verye plenteously in Essex and in Kent, and in Bark shyre, but I could never see it in Germany.

Warner simply writes: 'Knee Holly or Butcher's Broom. In the woody parts of the Forest. Found near Woodford Row, in great plenty: common.' In 1898 F. W. Elliott had this to say about it: 'Fairly common, seldom bearing fruit, not likely to become rare, since its roots are very deep, sending up fresh shoots every year' (*Essex Naturalist*).

The quaint *Ruscus*, once widely used as a miniature brush for sweeping out the grocery store and butcher's shop, is still fairly common on the Forest. Two specimens in my garden, from a friend's hedge bordering the Forest, produce flowers. This plant is of separate sex, and the female plant bears bright red berries each autumn. The peculiarity about *Ruscus* is the position of the tiny flowers which appear to emerge from the centre of the leaf, as mentioned by Turner. Actually these are not leaves, but modified branches called *cladodes*, which take on the function of leaves. Before berries appear it would seem necessary to have male and female plants in close proximity.

The mistletoe was in Turner's day more closely linked with the bird by its spelling of 'misseltoe':

> The best missel byrde lyme is made of a certain rounde fruyte that groweth in an oake; the leafe of the bush that beareth it, is lyke unto boxe. It groweth also in apple and crab trees and peare trees and other trees and sometyme at the routes of some bushes . . . This Missel doth grow no other ways, but by ye sede in such places whereas byrdes have devoured the fruyt, and have discharged it in the tre. I never sawe more plentye of righte oke miscel, then Hugh Moran showed me in London. It was sent to hym out of Essex . . . where as there is more plentye than in anye place of Englande I have been in.

Today, wherever the mistletoe happens to survive in Britain, it appears to have deserted the oak tree, its traditional host in the pre-Christian days of Druidism. Warner in his *Plantae*, however, records it 'on trees, particularly the oak, apple, pear, ash, lime, willow, elm, etc. etc. Found on an oak, between Woodford Row and the Bald Faced Stag, near the ten mile Stone: and on an apple tree in an orchard in Loughton; and on several trees, many of them oaks, between that place and Mr. Conyer's, Copped Hall'.

Elliott (1898) wrote: 'Viscum album. On the crab apple. I have not seen it south of Debden Slade . . . as I have never seen any large bunches in the Forest I fear that somebody cuts it, mistletoe being a marketable commodity.'

Butcher's broom and mistletoe—the one still with us but the other, alas, no more—are but two of the flowering plants to be found in the early Forest records (see Bibliography).

# 13

# THE FLOWERLESS PLANTS

*Ophioglossum*—Adder's toonge . . . groweth in moist meadowes throughout most parts of Englande, as in the fields in Waltham forrest.

John Gerard. Herball (1597)

In Epping Forest the trees, such as oak, beech and hornbeam, overshadow the woodland scene. Below this is a subordinate layer of smaller trees and shrubs, such as hawthorn, holly and bramble. Then, at ground level, comes a herb layer of grasses and flowering herbs, such as the wood soft grass, the bluebell and wood sorrel. These constitute the growth layers of plants in an English woodland (see page 82).

It is the lowest layer, called the Bryophyte zone, which can easily be overlooked, even ignored. In it will be found the lowly flowerless plants, such as algae, mosses, liverworts, lichens, fungi and ferns. Each belongs to a separate group of the plant kingdom, as much part of the woodland community as the tall trees which dominate it from above. Indeed, many derive benefit from the shelter and shade of the leaf canopy, and thrive in damp, dark places. This is partly the reason why they can compete with the woodland flowers. When the bluebell, primrose, anemone and other woodland flowers have blossomed and set their seeds by mid-summer, the mosses, ferns and fungi take over. Fruiting mostly in autumn, they are then at their best, even well into a mild winter.

We have a good knowledge and record of these flowerless plants of the Forest, due largely to the patient search and study made by a few enthusiasts who have specialised in one or other of these neglected groups. High on the list or such devotees is Miss Giulielma Lister (see page 163), who made an exhaustive survey of the mysterious Myxomycetes, or slime fungi. These are the small dots and patches of jelly-like substance, often attractively coloured in reds, white or blues, which appear in damp spots, usually on bare wood, such as a tree-stump, fallen log or branch, or a wooden fence. These 'Myxies' are a strange tribe of fungoid growth. The main body structure is called a plasmodium, out of which appear the brightly coloured sporangia. Slime fungi have two animal-like characteristics: they 'feed' on the organic matter of the wood, and they can slowly move their position by a kind of creeping growth.

Even more curious perhaps are the symbiotic lichens. This descriptive word, meaning a 'living together', is what happens in these lowly organisms, for a lichen plant is a combination of a fungus and an alga. Whereas some of the algal species found in lichens can also live independently, the fungi cannot do so. It is thought that by photosynthesis the alga makes food from which the fungus profits. In any case the algal cells embedded inside a covering of fungal threads are well protected and kept moist. It is the fungus which produces the fruiting bodies in the shape of tiny cups, often brightly coloured.

Lichens appear to lead a spartan life and can exist on bare rock in the bleakest surroundings; in a woodland area like the Forest one would expect to see them growing on bark and branches of trees as epiphytes, on old walls and palings of neighbouring houses and gardens, or as colonisers on burnt ground. A peaty soil in particular is bound to attract them as the first arrivals. However, there are two essentials: they must have plenty of light and pure air if they are to thrive. It is air pollution more than anything which has caused the disappearance of many of the Forest lichens over the past 100 years or so. Whereas at one time oaks, beeches and hornbeams were festooned and bearded with a greyish covering of lichens, there is now little to be found on the bare trunks.

Page *139* (*above*) the great diving beetle (*Dytiscus*) inhabits Forest ponds; (*below*) butcher's broom with flowers which will turn into red berries

Page 140 (above) Female common frog with spawn laid the day before; (below) the Forest pond by the Earl's Path, Loughton, formerly a gravel pit

As far back as 1883, the Rev James Crombie, a lichenologist and member of the Essex Field Club, deplored the loss of the Forest lichens. In the *Essex Naturalist* he mentions the collections of forty species made by Edward Forster, and deposited with the British Museum. To this he added his own finds to make a total of some 170 species and varieties. Since his day there has been a decline in the number of species, due to the destruction of old trees (lichens are slow growers so exist best on old trees), and to lack of light in the many shaded areas. Crombie speaks of the pollution and smoke carried across from the Lea Valley factories which were noticeable even in his day. He writes:

> Such causes as these are tending in the diminution of the lichen flora of the Forest, and were probably more or less at work in the days of Forster; but there can be no question that of recent years [1880s] they have been much more actively and extensively in operation. It will therefore be very interesting for the biochemist of the future—some fifty or a hundred years hence—to compare the above list of lichens with those that the Forest may then present.

Here indeed is a challenge for some modern Forest lichenologist, for little work has been carried out of recent years on this interesting plant group.

Whereas lichens prefer the drier places, the bryophytes, composed of mosses and liverworts, can more readily be found in the damp parts of the Forest. The two groups can usually be distinguished from one another by their build. Usually a liverwort, or hepatic, grows as a flat, somewhat oval structure, having a superficial resemblance to a tiny lettuce leaf. This is called a *thallus*, and a whole spreading colony may be found growing on damp mud or some tree-root, stone or wall, close to the ground in a sheltered place. A moss plant tends to grow in the upright position, and supports a number of leaves. A patch of moss is really a whole colony of individual plants. A single plant is only noticeable when a moss patch is pulled apart.

Mosses and liverworts are much more in evidence than lichens, and lists have been recorded from time to time (see Bibliography). Perhaps these need bringing up to date—a job that awaits an enterprising bryologist. Quite apart from this there is also the pleasure of getting to know these attractive plants more closely.

In his *Epping Forest* Buxton lists ninety-two species of moss, including *Zygodon forsteri* (mentioned on page 162). The following three species, each in different habitats, should not be hard to find. One of these, the cushion moss, *Leucobryum glaucum*, grows in mounds under the beech trees. In dry summers it dries out and bleaches almost white, but after continuous rain and especially towards autumn it colours an attractive green, making quite a picture under the bronze canopy of beech leaves. The bog moss, *Sphagnum*, grows in wet hollows on acid soil, forming rose coloured tufts. This, too, dries out when exposed and becomes almost white. It readily absorbs water and revives. This moss was once extensively used as a form of absorbent bandage or covering, and today serves as packing material for plants in transit. A third common species, the hair moss, *Polytrichum*, is found on the heath areas, growing in company with the bracken and heather on the acid soils. Dense patches of it soon appear on burnt ground after a Forest fire.

Ferns grow to a larger size and should be more readily spotted during a Forest ramble. Unfortunately, they are all too few in number, apart from the ubiquitous bracken. A survey carried out by R. M. Payne for the London Natural History Society covers an area taking in the old Forest limits from Forest Gate in the south, to Nazeing and North Weald in the north. This meant searching in a number of outlying woods which once formed part of the more extensive Forest of Waltham. Payne's list covers nineteen species of ferns, two now being extinct from the district. Of all the Forest localities, the Lower Forest, or Wintry Wood, is the most productive. Here the male fern, *Dryopteris felix-mas*, is quite common, as it also is in the extreme south, in Wanstead Park. Wintry Wood also harbours the broad buckler fern, *Dryopteris dilatata*, and the graceful lady fern, *Athyrium felix-faemina*. Here, too, the common polypody, *Polypodium vulgare*, can occasionally be seen in the crown of a pollarded hornbeam or oak. This was once a widespread feature of the Forest flora. Here and there on old walls of neighbouring gardens can be found an occasional species of spleenwort (*Asplenium*), including the wall rue, *Asplenium ruta-muraria*. Oddly enough, the bracken, *Pteris aquilinum*, is mostly absent from the Lower Forest, preferring the more gravelly soils. It occurs extensively in the glades and along the rides among the birches in the Wake Arms and High Beech area.

One of the most interesting of the Forest ferns is the small and primitive adder's tongue, *Ophioglossum vulgatum*. Its spore-bearing stem has a tongue-like appearance, although not particularly like that of a snake. To its base is attached a single, blade-shaped frond. This curious little fern grows shyly in a number of places between Chingford and Loughton, usually in long grass half-hidden beneath thorn bushes and in various glades.

The few fern species left to us make a link with the distant past for they existed in abundance before the flowers arrived on the scene, in the Carboniferous Period—the age of coal. This is even more true of those 'living fossils' called horsetails which can be found growing in damp hollows or beside the Forest ditches and ponds. Nature's gift of coal comes from the fossilised remains of the Equisitales which flourished in vast forests some 250 million years ago. In one little valley in the Forest every summer there appears a dense mass of horsetails which, in imagination, can be likened to a coal age forest in miniature. Fossilised remains of both fern and horsetail from the coal seams show that some of these plants have hardly changed in all these millions of years.

# 14
# FUNGI

Fungi ben mussherons . . . there be two manners of them, one
manner is deedly and sleeth them that eateth of them and be
called tode stoles, and the other doeth not.
The Grete Herball (1526)

Whatever claim to fame Epping Forest may have as a naturalist's
hunting ground, it is undoubtedly renowed for its fungi, and has
been described by Dr J. Ramsbottom, a leading British mycologist, as 'probably the best worked area for its size in the world'.
This is largely due to the activities of the Essex Field Club
which, on 2 October 1880, held its first field meeting in Monk
Wood. Needless to say the main attraction for that time of the
year was the numerous toadstools and other fungi to be found
and gathered during the ramble. This outing, attended by fifty
members and led by Dr Cooke, was a success despite the heavy
rain. Some sixty species of fungi were found, and one of the
members is said to have used his open umbrella as a container for
specimens. From this meeting was born the kind of naturalists'
outing known today as a 'fungus foray'. In the club's report the
recorder has this to say: 'How frequently we have the enquiry
from incipient naturalists "what shall I study and how shall I
begin?" Those who attended this meeting had both precept and
example to divert their choice.' It then goes on to describe the
Club's first outing:

> . . . and how much there is of interest in the history, but very
> partially known, of that mysterious tribe called Fungi by the
> learned, and toadstools, mushrooms and moulds by the general.

Flowerless they are by name and nature but often of striking beauty. A search in Epping Forest any fine morning in this present month of October will reveal many a cryptogamic gem; the brilliant Fly Agaric with its scarlet crown, etc . . . Here then is a hobby attractive and comparatively unridden and our Forest is the very place in which to exercise it, Epping being perhaps one of the best known localities for the larger Fungi in England.

The Club's second foray, on 1 October 1881, was attended by over 100 members, this time in pleasant sunshine. It included an amusing incident. One member turned up with a rather unconventional lunch consisting of slices of beef-steak bracket fungus, *Fistulina hepatica*, sandwiched between bread, and garnished with fiery tasting bits of the milky toadstool, *Lactarius piperatus*. He consumed this before an admiring audience!

Fungi, which are lacking in chlorophyll, must seek their food in organic form, as in the case of animals, and do so mainly by living on the dead remains of other plants. These are the so-called saprophytes which grow in leafmould, on dead trees, branches, logs and stumps. The actual fungus plant is hidden within the wood or leafmould, in the form of a mass of fine threads, called a *mycelium*. This is the same as the mushroom 'spawn' of the edible fungus. From this emerges, in the fruiting season, the visible part of the fungus, usually in the mild and damp period of late summer and autumn. From this structure, called the *sporophore*, are liberated the huge quantities of minute spores, any one of which, carried off by the wind, could settle somewhere and germinate into a new fungus.

By far the commonest shape in sporophores is the typical toadstool with its umbrella cap and circle of gills underneath, supported on a stalk. All such gilled toadstools belong to the large group called the Agaricales. They will probably turn up in numbers more than any of the other fungus groups. Among them are included some of the more dangerous species, belonging mainly to the genus *Amanita*. These are the so-called 'perfect' toadstools, in which both ring and volva are present. Gills are pure white and the cap is covered in spots. The deadly death cap, *Amanita phalloides*, occasionally turns up in the Forest, usually half hidden under a bush. Much more conspicuous is the brilliant fly agaric, *A. muscaria*, mentioned in the Field Club's report above, and so named from the old custom of using it as a fly-killer by cutting up pieces in milk. This handsome fungus must be looked for under Forest birches, growing among the bracken patches.

Many other agarics will turn up during a ramble; with a little practice and the aid of a field guide, these can be identified and, in some cases, put aside for the frying pan. Doreen Boardman, the Woodford botanist, has assisted me on many forays in naming the various species and she now keeps the Forest record for the Essex Field Club. The list of larger fungi is approaching 800, with new discoveries turning up almost every year.

In addition to the Amanitas there are other fungi with distinctive features to search for. The *Boletus* toadstools are of a robust build with a spongy under-surface in place of gills, covered in pores through which their spores are shed. Among these is a popular edible species, *Boletus edulis*, called the *Cépe* in France and *Steinpilz* in Germany.

The bracket fungi, Polyporaceae, grow from dead or dying trees, and often are specific to a certain tree. Such is the case with the birch polypore, *Polyporus betulinus*, which is easy to find. Less common is the striking blood red beef-steak fungus, *Fistulina hepatica*, on oak. Curious rounded earthballs of the family Sclerodermaceae growing on hidden tree roots could be mistaken for large pebbles. These should not be confused with the puff-balls, Lycoperdaceae, which puff out little clouds of spores when touched or struck by rain drops.

Little fairy clubs or stag's-horn fungi, Clavariaceae, peep out of the grass or grow on tree stumps, and tiny saucer-shaped pixie-cups, Pezizaceae, hide against the bare soil, especially in burnt places. They take a little searching after, but the stinkhorn, *Phallus impudicus*, may be tracked down by its smell. With some luck one may possibly find a specimen of the odd-shaped bird's-nest fungus, *Crucibulum*, or maybe one of the earthstars, *Geaster*. Occasionally a gourmet's delicacy, such as a truffle, has been found in the Forest.

During the Field Club's third foray, in 1882, a specimen of *Elaphomyces granulatus* was picked up just below the Loughton camp in Monk Wood, at the very spot where some commoners' pigs were out grubbing for food. At one time pigs and dogs were trained to find these hidden fungi. The author well remembers attending the autumn forays of the Essex Field Club during the 1930s, at which 100 or more enthusiasts might turn out. At the end of the ramble we would gather at one of the Forest tea-houses to sort out and identify the collection by displaying them in rows on plates to make an impressive display. Today many other societies and groups follow the example of the Field Club by visiting Epping Forest for a 'foray among the fungusses'.

# 15
# TREES AND SHRUBS

The Oak's Pedigree
In my great gransire's trunk did Druids dwell,
My grandsire with the Roman eagle fell,
Myself a sapling when my father bore,
The new Edward to the gaelic shore.

ANON

The expression that 'one cannot see the wood for the trees' does not fully apply to Epping Forest. Such may be true of the monotonous ranks of a single species of conifer in a state forest or endless rows of fruit trees in an orchard. The Forest is much more broken up by glades, patches of heath and common, and by a variation of trees and shrubs which act more as a backcloth to the scene. A selection of these trees and shrubs is given here, accompanied by quotations from Warner's *Plantae* and from a list compiled by F. W. Elliott for the *Essex Naturalist* in 1898.

Oak, beech, hornbeam and birch are the main Forest trees. Oak and hornbeam are undoubted natives since prehistoric times; birch is an invader, whereas beech is somewhat of a mystery. At least, nobody has given a satisfactory explanation as to its widespread presence. Two species of oak are recognised as being native to Britain. These are the common or pedunculate oak, *Quercus robor* (= *pedunculata*) and the sessile oak, *Quercus petraea* (= *sessiliflora*). The former is better suited to the richer and heavier soils found more in the south and lowlands, such as the London Clay which fills the Thames Basin, and on which most of the Forest lies. The acorn cup is attached to the tree by a stalk. The sessile oak belongs more to the poorer, more acid, soil of the north and west of the country, and on the uplands. The acorn cup sits directly on the tree branch without a stalk.

Warner described them in this manner: 'The Common Oak. In woods, the woody parts of the Forest, and in hedges: common.' The other species he calls, 'The Oak Trees with the acorns on short foot stalks. As the former. Found on the Forest between Muncombe and the Bald-faced Stag: not common.' In this he is quite correct, that the stalked *Q. robor* is the common Forest oak. Elliott writes of it growing elsewhere, on moist as well as dry ground, being more plentiful on the heavy clay because the beech is not there to smother it. He mentions that there are many forms, loosely grouped under three varieties: *pubescens, sessiliflora* and *pedunculata*. He quotes Warner, and also Buxton (1923), who for some reason states that the oak which abounds in the Forest is the variety *sessiliflora* 'having its acorns without footstalks'. Elliott challenges this and has no hesitation in saying that 'the great many oaks in the Forest may be broadly classed under *pedunculata*'.

The oak looks its best in May, especially if there is a heavy blooming of the pendulous male catkins. This, together with the flush of young leaves, gives the tree a creamy green look. The hum of bees when gathering pollen can be quite loud on a quiet day. Later on, in a good fruiting year, the ground becomes littered with acorns, a feast for deer, squirrel, jay, and formerly the commoners' pigs. Of all Forest trees, the oak was perhaps the most prized 'vert', valued by commoner and Crown alike. Today it would grow best in the wetter parts, such as the Lower Forest or on Fairmead Bottom, away from competition with the beech.

The beech, *Fagus sylvaticus*, is my favourite Forest tree. Although largely pollarded in most places, there are a few untouched groves here and there, especially along the Green Ride in Monk Wood, and through Epping Thicks. There is some evidence to suggest that this part of the Forest within the Manor of Waltham was given protection from the axe by the monks of the great abbey. Little grows under beech trees, owing to a dense shady canopy of spreading leaves during the summer season. This is part of the charm of a beech wood, since the view is not obstructed by undergrowth, and one can see well ahead through the tree trunks. There is nothing more attractive in Forest scenery, to my mind, than the delicate pale green of young beech leaves against the metallic grey bark of the smooth trunks. The ground is a thick brown carpet of crisp dried leaves. In autumn the whole tree turns a rich bronze and the woodland floor is splashed with green patches of cushion-moss, and bright dots of colour where the toadstools are fruiting. Elliott says, 'This, our most beautiful tree, is happily plentiful on all high ground, but it does not like cold wet soils.'

Like the oak, the beech has its good and poor seasons, and occasionally provides a feast of nuts for squirrel, woodmouse, finch and tit. It attracts certain kinds of fungi which grow on or beneath it. The argument as to the correct spelling of the Forest's highest spot—High Beech or High Beach—is a perennial one. There is a layer of Bagshot sand at this level, a kind of beach, but there are also some fine beech trees on the hill opposite the church, overlooking Fairmead Plain. The author prefers the former spelling, as used by Richard Warner.

The hornbeam, *Carpinus betulus*, is recorded by Warner as, 'The Horn, or Hard-beam Tree, called in some places, the Horse-beech or Horn-beech, from some likeness of the leaves to the Beech. In all parts of the Forest, and in hedges: very common.' Epping Forest has been described as the last hornbeam forest in Britain. This tree has certainly played its role in Forest history. It was much favoured by the commoners, since it readily recovered after periodic lopping, could grow on wet as well as dry soil, and provided excellent wood for fuel and carpentry. Many an axe or spade handle, or spoke of a cartwheel, was made from this hardwood. The charcoal made from hornbeam timber went to the gunpowder mills; here and there, traces of the firing pits of the old charcoal-burners can still be found. These hardy folk would live on the spot, night and day, so as to keep watch and control over the burning wood. This should not burst into flame, but remain smouldering to the last ember. A correspondent to the *Illustrated London News* wrote in 1879: 'The appearance of a burning heap, with jets of flame and puffs of smoke issuing from many crevices in its sides, cannot easily be forgotten by those who have seen it at night.' Hornbeam may be recognised by its smooth, streakily marked bark, hanging flower catkins which sometimes festoon the branches, followed by crops of nutlets, each with a curious three-lobed wing. The leaves, which resemble those of the beech, have a toothed border and are strongly veined. This tree gets its name from the wooden yoke, or hornbeam, at one time used for harnessing oxen to the plough or waggon.

Silver birch, *Betula alba*, the most graceful of Forest trees, is deservedly called 'the Lady of the Woods'. Elliott records three sub-species: '*verrucosa* of graceful shape with pendulous branches; *glutinosa* with stiffer habit and denser foliage, and *pubescens* which looks similar to *glutinosa* and has twigs and leaves covered with a denser and velvety down'. Modern botanists recognise two separate species of birch in Britain:

Silver Birch, *Betula verrucosa*. Three of graceful shape with pendulous branches, papery bark in black and white, trunk rugged at base, twigs shiny brown, hairless but often covered with tiny warts. Leaves pointed, oval, toothed irregularly, becoming yellow in autumn. Fruit with two wings twice as broad as the seed. Prefers sandy and gravelly soils on heaths, especially in south.
Downy or Common Birch, *Betula pubescens*. Tree more stiff in shape, branches more erect, bark greyish brown, base of trunk not rugged. Twigs darker, downy and dull. Leaves less narrowly pointed with more regular teeth. Fruit with wings as broad as seed. Prefers wetter conditions, more common in Scotland, and at higher altitudes.

The two species may be confused as there are many hybrids. The silver birch is by far the more common of the two in the Forest.

Since it is a rapid coloniser it will be interesting to see whether it takes over completely the present open spaces in the various glades, and where fires have occurred, especially around High Beech church and the Wake Arms crossroads where it is now firmly entrenched. Indeed, Buxton's prophecy appears to be coming true:

> Formerly it [the Birch] was not common in the Forest, but, from the enormous production of seeds which are carried far on the wind by the little wing attached to them, it is spreading itself rapidly, and I anticipate that, in a comparatively short period, it will to some extent supplant the other trees. Wherever a clearance has been made, either intentionally or by accidental fires, if the soil be dry, it appears to spring up spontaneously. The rough open ground by High Beech Church has been quite recently covered by a charming grove of birches which have probably sown themselves from the neighbouring areas . . . The same is taking place in the open plain to the north of the Theydon Road. Those who are now middle-aged will live to see the bare plain between the Wake Arms and Monk Wood . . . similarly restored by nature.

This was written in the first edition of his *Epping Forest*, in 1884. In my own lifetime, from the late 1920s, when I first started exploring the Forest, I have seen the steady spread of these beautiful but prolific trees across 'the open plain to the north of the Theydon Road', which is called Long Running. The other plain, between the Wake Arms and Monk Wood, is now almost entirely covered with a pure stand of silver birch.

# 16

# WATERWAYS AND PONDS

Venator: 'There is also a little fish called a Sticklebag, a fish without scales, but hath his body fenced with several prickles. I know not where he dwells in winter; nor what he is good for in summer, but only to make sport for boys and women-anglers . . .'

IZAAK WALTON. *The Compleat Angler*

The ancient Forest of Waltham, what is left of it today, lies on the watershed in a long and narrow crescent between two northern tributaries of the Thames, the Lea and Roding. The Forest heights are drained by side streams which eventually find their way across fields, once part of the Forest, to the flowing rivers. These river valleys were the first places to become settled and occupied by man (see page 14).

There can be little doubt that the rivers and their fertile slopes have had a big influence on Forest history, and indirectly on its wildlife. In the 2,000-year interval between the Iron Age villager and the modern City commuter, the scene along the Lea and Roding valleys has greatly changed. Where once there were reed beds and willows, clear waters, trout, beaver and bittern, today much of the landscape has been obliterated by the creeping fingers of London's suburbia. The river banks have been straightened and leveed to prevent winter flooding, and the riverside vegetation destroyed. The marshes have been drained, although their names still exist. Pollution from factory waste and chemicals used on the land is a constant hazard. The heavy demand on the water supply has lowered the water table, so that the rivers become dangerously low during drought periods. Most of the old wells, such as Woodford Wells, are now dry, and the Forest spas but a memory.

All these demands on a river have brought about changes in the landscape and wildlife. One thinks ruefully of the days, not so long ago, when Izaak Walton sat on the bank of his beloved Lea, in conversation with his friend Venator. There were still trout to be had, and salmon entered the Thames until 1833. The presence of such cold-water northern fish is a sign of pure and healthy water courses in which they can spawn. Fringed with reed beds, willow and water meadows, the two Forest rivers must have presented an atmosphere and beauty worthy of a Constable painting. One has visions of all sorts of exciting things to be seen in company with Walton. His *Compleat Angler* contains many references to fish and fowl, and in old documents one learns of such treasures as swallowtail butterflies flitting about the Hackney marshes, or otters penetrating the Roding as far as Wanstead Park.

### RESERVOIRS

The Lea Valley now contains a string of reservoirs which provide part of London's water supply. An essential service demanded by a civilised society is the constant supply of pure water. The storage reservoir is the first stage in this process. From here the water passes through the filter beds to remove any microscopic impurities, and so to the consumer. The advantage of a reservoir is in creating a reserve supply of water which, unlike river water, is static. Any particles of mud, etc, carried in suspension by a river, will sink in the reservoir. Such sedimentation helps to clear the water. Much of it at Walthamstow has been carried down from the fertile chalk hills to the north. It is the richness of mineral salts, coupled with the open aspect of the reservoir water to sun and sky, that encourages a build-up of those minute plants, the algae.

Apart from diatoms and other algae, the reservoirs teem with small drifting animal life, such as the water flea (*Daphnia*) and its

154

allies. The reservoirs are well stocked with carp, roach, pike and bream, which in turn attract the fish-hunting birds, such as the heron. The phyto-plankton not only enriches the water with ample supplies of oxygen, but provides food for the *Daphnia* and midge larvae, which in turn feed the fish.

Angling is permitted and the tolerant water board officials allow visits by parties of bird-watchers who have learned much about the comings and goings of water birds, especially during winter. Over a hundred grebes have been counted in the Lea Valley during one season.

One of the more spectacular sights on the reservoirs takes place every winter evening just before dark. This is the arrival of thousands of the so-called 'London gull'. This is the black-headed gull in winter plumage, which began to winter inland about eighty years ago, especially in and around the larger cities of western Europe. As a scavenger it spends the daytime in London parks, along Thames-side, on open sports fields and golf links, and on rubbish dumps. Then, as dusk falls, gulls can be seen flying out of London towards their roosts on the reservoirs. Those making for the Lea Valley cross the inner suburbs of Wanstead, Leytonstone and Woodford, heading towards Walthamstow. A count of gulls on the No 5 reservoir in 1954 amounted to some 35,000 on one occasion. In all there are up to 100,000 gulls of various species roosting around London during the winter nights.

There was an interesting interim period, during which the reservoirs were being built. The excavations exposed large areas of Thames gravel which remained dry and uncovered before flooding began. This turned out to be ideal territory for a number of ground-feeding and nesting birds, such as the skylark, wagtail, lapwing and some waders. It was during the building of the new William Girling reservoir at Chingford, in 1947, that an interesting discovery was made. Four pairs of the little ringed plover were recorded. This dainty little wader, normally confined to pebbly beaches along the coast, has also been seen in a number of gravel pits.

The Forest rivers and streams still provide an attractive habitat for many creatures, from the homely moorhen to the occasional otter or kingfisher, despite the constant threat from pollution and drainage. What may have been lost from the actual rivers has largely been compensated for by the man-made reservoirs and ponds.

POND LIFE

Many a naturalist can trace his hobby or profession back to that first adventure which took him to his local pond. As a young pond-dipper, armed with jam-jar and sixpenny net, I used to return home with many treasures found in some Forest pond, little aware that I was contravening the bye-law. All the wildlife, big and small, plant and animal, is protected on Forest ground, and permission should be sought before collecting specimens. My keenness to collect and to understand more about pond life is perhaps understandable, since a pond can become a source of endless discovery and interest. A very large variety of animals and water plants from many different groups make up the pond community, and there is no better outdoor classroom for a young naturalist to visit.

Ponds in Epping Forest are all of artificial origin; many were created in the last century when much gravel digging took place in order to supply surfacing for the roadway then being built, before tar macadam came into general use. Where the Thames river gravels and glacial deposits occur will be found clusters of these ponds, usually near roads. The four main groups are on Wanstead and Leytonstone Flats; along the main road between Whipp's Cross and Woodford Wells; on Strawberry Hill by Earl's Path, just outside Loughton; and along Ranger's Road by Chingford Plain. At the time of these digging operations there was much protest from Forest lovers and naturalists. For instance, in 1893 the *Essex Naturalist* reported that 'at the side of the Earl's Path between High Beach and Loughton a large quantity of gravel has been excavated to a depth of 15 feet', and went on to deplore the unsightly nature of such bare exposures within the Forest. Today, far from being an eyesore, these same ponds are scenes of much natural beauty during the summer months.

Another type of pond has formed through arresting the natural flow of one of the Forest streams. These drain the area by flowing off the watershed between the valleys of the rivers Lea and Roding into which they discharge their contents. Where some kind of solid barrier, such as a road or ride, has been built across a stream, the water piles up against the obstruction. Two examples are Baldwin's Pond and the Wake Valley Pond.

Other ponds were built for ornamental purposes by owners of private property before it was acquired by the conservators. Such are the ponds and lakes in Wanstead Park, Higham's Park and Knighton Wood. A fourth group of ponds came into existence during World War II, when a number of large bombs and parachute mines fell on Forest soil, fortunately away from habitation, leaving craters in the London Clay which filled up with rain water.

At the present day there are over 100 ponds in the Forest area, not to mention the water ditches and innumerable water-filled hollows and puddles. The preservation of any water locality should be a matter of priority in wildlife conservation, since it can so easily be reclaimed and disappear in course of time by a natural process of invasion from the bankside.

To list the inhabitants of the Forest ponds would be boring and also incomplete, since new species are always turning up for the district. Adult stages of some aquatic insects are capable of flight and move about from one area to the next. Forest naturalists have studied and duly recorded species from different groups, and published lists on behalf of their respective societies, such as the Essex Field Club, the London Natural History Society, and the Queckett Microscopical Society. The last of these, one of the oldest amateur societies in the country, specialises in the study of the smaller forms of pond life. Around the turn of the century many keen microscopists searched the Forest ponds and pools for their microscopic contents, of which even a temporary puddle could yield a treasure or two. Buxton, in his *Epping Forest*, includes a chapter with some interesting details contributed by Dr M. C. Cooke of the Essex Field Club. Among the minute plants he refers to are the unicellular algae which can turn still water green when massed together. Of these, the desmids, some fifty species, are the most attractive under the lens. Filamentous algae, up to thirty species, consist of cells growing end to end as fine threads. Massed and tangled together, they produce the clouds of green and often slimy plant growth popularly called 'blanket-weed'. Often unsightly and associated with unpleasant odours of stagnant water, they are, when seen under the microscope, attractively coloured and designed.

Some 100 species of one-celled animals, called Protozoa, have been identified, including a number of species of the well-known Amoeba. Hydrozoa, the freshwater cousins of sea anemones, include the fascinating little hydra, both green and brown kinds. Rotifers, or wheel animalcules, are those strange little creatures with rings of cilia at one end. These beat in rhythmic fashion, giving the impression of miniature catherine wheels. Of the 150 species in the Forest, some are fixed and others free-swimming.

Polyzoa, or 'moss' animals, consist of colonies of tiny hydralike animals attached like mossy growths to water plants and the shells of snails and water beetles. Among the Crustacea, which are mainly a marine group, such as crabs and lobsters, there are a number of small freshwater forms. These are the familiar *Daphnia* group, or water fleas, so-called because of their jerky movements. These and their allies, such as *Cyclops* and *Cypris*, up to a 100 or so species, make up the drifting plankton of the Forest ponds, on which the larger animals feed.

Water insects are well in evidence during the summer days, and soon colonise new areas if they can fly, as happened to the water-filled bomb craters after the war. Water beetles, dragonflies, numerous mosquitoes and their allies come and go, as do the temporary visitors, the amphibians. Common frog and common toad meet in their spawning groups each spring, so that tadpoles are amply represented by early summer. All three

158

British species of newts occur, although the largest crested newt, *Triturus cristatus*, is now somewhat of a rarity. For these interesting animals alone ponds are an essential need to their survival.

Apart from the ubiquitous stickleback, a fair selection of fish occur, some being introduced from time to time to supply the fishing interests. Carp, tench, bream, roach, rudd, perch, pike and gudgeon are the species which an angler might anticipate in his catch. There are some fine specimens of Forest caught fish, especially carp, in the museum at the Hunting Lodge, Chingford.

# 17

# FOREST NATURALISTS AND THEIR WORK

In 1771, Gilbert White wrote to his friend Thomas Pennant: '. . . a natural history of my native parish, an *annus historico naturalis* comprising a journal be compiled for a whole year and illustrated with large notes and diagrams. Such a beginning might induce more able naturalists to write the history of various districts and might occasion the production of work so much to be wished for—a full and complete natural history of these kingdoms.'

*Natural History and Antiquities of Selborne* (1789)

Because of a close proximity to London, as well as its preserved state as a piece of undisturbed countryside, Epping Forest has attracted its fair share of naturalists over the years. At first these were individuals who, like the great pioneer Gilbert White of Selborne, were content to wander about by themselves through the woods and glades, in order to observe, collect and record their findings. Some of the more outstanding are mentioned here.

Among the earliest to record the Forest's wildlife was Richard Warner (1713–75). The son of a banker, at the age of nine Richard came with his mother to live at the house called Harts on Woodford Row. This Georgian residence is today used as a hospital. A man of private means, Warner gave most of his time to his garden, also to dancing and literary works. His garden attracted much attention and John Ellis, who paid him a visit one day in 1758, wrote to Linnaeus in Sweden, telling the great Flower King that he had seen Warner's:

. . . rare plant like a jasmine with a large double flower, very odiferous, which he received four years ago from the Cape of Good Hope. The flowers are so large that the specimen which he gave me to dissect was four inches across from the extremities of the limb. If you find the plant to be not a Jasmine but an undescribed genus, you will oblige me by calling it *Warneria* after its worthy possessor.

Some days later Ellis was obliged to write again: 'Mr Warner begs of me to write to you not to call it Warneria.' Eventually Linnaeus called it *Gardenia*. In Britain this well-known flower bloomed for the first time in Warner's garden at Woodford. This gentleman is best known to naturalists for his famous record of Forest plants, called *Plantae Woodfordiensis*. It was printed in 1771 at his own expense for private circulation among friends, of whom twenty-two are mentioned in the preface. Regular 'herborisations' made by his friends and students in the neighbourhood of Harts brought in numbers of records, and these were probably collated by Warner as he received them.

To a modern botanist the book is a little disappointing in that the localities for many of the plants are not given, or are vague. There was no Ordnance Survey map scheme or grid reference in Warner's day, and he speaks of a find 'by the Woodford bridge road near to the eight mile stone' or 'in the wood called the Hawk'. Historically speaking, however, the contents are fascinating to read. This is a collector's piece and anyone possessing a copy is fortunate. One can make comparisons between the flowers of Warner's day with those still existing after 200 years. There are some interesting names used for the plants, as well as differing spelling of familiar place names.

We turn next to the three Forster brothers, sons of a City merchant, Edward Forster the 'Elder', who settled in Walthamstow in 1764. His keen enthusiasm as a gardener and nature lover must have encouraged his sons to take up botany. Each had a copy of Warner's *Plantae Woodfordiensis*, rebound so as to contain extra blank pages on which each brother could add his own notes. The eldest, Thomas Furley Forster (1761–1825) left the district on his marriage and had little to contribute to Forest botany, apart from a few additions to Warner's list. As a matter of interest a moss was named after him, called *Zygodon forsteri* (see page 142). The second son, Benjamin Meggott (1764–1829) remained single. His notes on Forest flowers made in his copy of the *Plantae* are of considerable value, especially to those districts such as Walthamstow and Woodford which are now so heavily built up. Forster queries some of Warner's records, and is to be relied on far more since he made a collection of Forest plants, which still exists intact. His herbarium is preserved in the Botany Department of the Natural History Museum at South Kensington, actually in the name of his younger brother. Edward Forster (1765–1849) did well as a botanist, becoming a Fellow of the Linnean Society, and eventually a vice-president. On the death of his father he moved to a house near Higham's Park. Like his brother Benjamin, Edward has his name perpetuated in a plant, the woodrush, *Luzula forsteri*. At one stage in his career, in 1843, Edward conceived the idea of writing up a county flora of Essex, and penned his thoughts to his friend Gibson. However, Gibson could find no such manuscript among Forster's effects, so he took on the task himself, as he mentions in the preface to his well-known work *Flora of Essex*, published in 1862.

Whereas Warner and the Forsters were primarily gardeners and botanists, Henry Doubleday (1808–75) was an entomologist. He was the elder son of an Epping grocer and provision merchant who started up a business in 1770. The family were Quakers and belonged to the Society of Friends. The proximity of the Forest no doubt stimulated Henry's interest in wildlife. Whereas his younger brother Edward left the district for higher things, becoming secretary to the Entomological Society of London and a member of the British Museum staff, Henry remained a grocer and amateur naturalist at Epping all his life. Helping with the business, and then taking over after his father's death in 1843, he still found time to devote to his hobby. He was a keen shot and excellent taxidermist, and early in life had amassed a collection of local birds which he mounted himself. It was Doubleday who first recorded for Britain the little ringed plover, a wader which caused a sensation around London not so long ago. He also observed the blue-headed wagtail, a race of the yellow wagtail. In 1843 he recorded in *The Zoologist* a number of bats found in the Forest. He also introduced the edible frog to a pond at Epping, and its nightly calls no doubt puzzled the nearby residents, as they did over 100 years later from a pond facing the Forest School at Snaresbrook. In 1947 the author's wife heard them croaking merrily from the roadside. None of the local people knew how they got there.

During a brief visit to Paris, Henry Doubleday was struck with the way in which the continental entomologists classified and named their insects. Back home he attempted to bring the English system into line with that abroad so as to make the two compatible. This took many years to achieve and became known as 'Doubleday's List', a valuable contribution to scientific classification.

Among the botanists who have pursued their studies in Epping Forest and district, probably the greatest of all was John Ray, of Black Notley in North Essex (1627–1705). He preceded the great Linnaeus in an attempt to classify plants by a somewhat cumbersome descriptive method. This was adopted by Richard Warner in his *Plantae*, examples of which appear in Chapter 12. More recently there was a much admired woman botanist who deserves mention here. Miss Giulielma Lister, FLS, niece of the famous surgeon Lord Lister, was born in Leytonstone and lived there all her life, well into her eighties. She collaborated with her father, Arthur Lister, in the compilation of a monograph on the strange and little studied Mycetozoa, or slime fungi, those curious but colourful excrescences which appear after wet weather on bare surfaces of tree trunks, wall and soil. Miss Lister carried on the work after her father's death in 1908, becoming a world authority. Most of her collecting was done in Epping Forest, in particular in Wanstead Park which during her lifetime became part of the Forest. She joined the Essex Field Club and became its first lady president in 1916. She was elected Fellow of the Linnean Society in 1904 and made vice-president in 1918. An abridged version of the Mycetozoa monograph was published by the Field Club in 1918 as one of its special memoirs. In this Miss Lister named eighty-eight species and varieties. Her collection was eventually given to the Natural History Museum.

In the study of the pre-historical world and the search for fossils, little work seems to have been done inside the Forest itself, but many former searchers have been rewarded with discoveries made in the gravels and clays along the Lea and Roding valleys which flank the woodlands. One of the outstanding names among these fossil collectors is that of Sir Antonio Brady (1811–81), who lived at Stratford. A civil servant with the Admiralty, he became known as the 'genial elephant hunter of the Roding valley'. It was in the neighbourhood of Ilford, in the Uphall brickfields, that masses of fossil elephant and other bones were extracted from the brick earth, a reddish Ice Age deposit. Well over 1,000 specimens were catalogued by Sir Antonio, and much of his material is with the national collection in the Natural History Museum, where a very fine skull of a mammoth, found at Ilford, is on public exhibition.

Apart from his fine contribution to the discovery and knowledge of the animals which roamed the Thames valley during the Ice Age, Sir Antonio played a prominent role in the fight to save the Forest. He founded the 'Forest Fund', and was elected a verderer. In 1871 he organised a public meeting on Wanstead Flats to protest against the threat of enclosure by the Trustees of Lord Cowley's estate.

It was towards the close of the last century that people in Britain interested in nature and the countryside began to band together into local societies whose aim was the study and recording of events and finds in their respective areas. Needless to say, Epping Forest attracted attention, and one of the country's first amateur groups was the Essex Field Club, originally named the 'Epping Forest and County of Essex Naturalists' Field Club'.

One summer's day in 1869, three naturalists, all out collecting butterflies, met in the Forest. From this chance meeting a friendship sprang up, out of which the Field Club was born. Each of these entomologists was elected an officer when the club was founded at a meeting held in Buckhurst Hill. Mr R. Meldola became president, Mr William Cole secretary, and Mr W. Angel librarian. Some eighty interested persons were enrolled to the club, and the Queen's Forest Ranger, the Duke of Connaught, was invited to become its patron. Two eminent naturalists, Charles Darwin and Alfred Wallace, who jointly founded the evolution theory, became honorary members. In 1882 the club's title was changed to the simpler 'Essex Field Club', as it is known today.

The club owns two museum collections composed largely of Epping Forest specimens, both on view to the public. One is housed at the Passmore Edwards Museum, next door to the West Ham Technical College in Romford, Stratford. This building was opened in October 1900, a venture made possible largely through the generous donation of £1,000 by Mr Passmore Edwards, a notable benefactor of his day. The other collection is housed in Queen Elizabeth's Hunting Lodge, the historic building on the outskirts of Chingford and the property of the City Corporation (see page 47). It was opened as a museum in November 1895. The collection was handed over to the Corporation in 1960.

The Essex Field Club publishes a journal, the *Essex Naturalist*, which contains the records of the club's indoor and outdoor meetings, as well as notes and papers from its members, a number of which are referred to in this book. From its inception, the club has made many records of the flora and fauna in Epping Forest. In his inaugural address at the club's foundation in February 1880, the president listed the following animals and plants discovered in the Forest: 7 species of bats, 118 birds, 12 ferns, 30 dragonflies and 11 mosses. From this modest start the club was soon to add impressive lists of other groups, such as insects, water life, fungi and flowers. The president did mention a number of flowering plants which were becoming rare, even in those days; twenty-four species were noted, of which nine were bog or marsh plants. He expressed the club's concern for these moisture-loving plants and its disapproval of the conservators' policy of drainage. The loss of boggy places would threaten the existence of these attractive flowers. This concern appears to have been well founded, for today some of these plants no longer survive in the Forest.

Another society to have close connections with the Forest is the London Natural History Society. This came into being in 1913 through an amalgamation of the City of London Entomological and Natural History Society, and the North London Natural History Society. This combination of forces, so to speak, was a wise move for it helped to strengthen and sustain the wildlife interests during the trying period of the war years. The LNHS, as it is usually called, has gone from strength to strength and now contains a number of sections in various branches of natural history. Its study area covers the London countryside within a radius of twenty miles of St Paul's. It publishes an annual journal, the *London Naturalist,* and the *London Bird Report.* The society has been active in Epping Forest since its inception, and now has an Epping Forest Field Section devoted to Forest rambles. Formerly there was also a Chingford and a Woodford branch.

Between 1942 and 1947 the Chingford branch carried out a survey of Forest wildlife in the region of the Cuckoo Pits and Peartree Plain. This lies in the St Thomas Quarters. The area studied measures 200 by 500yd and contains mixed woodland of oak and hornbeam, some rough grass and scrub on Peartree Plain, ten small pools and a small stream, the Cuckoo Brook. A report published in 1944 listed 122 flowering plants (including 10 tree species and 22 grasses), 33 mosses, 8 liverworts and 3 ferns. Birds numbered 64 species observed or heard, and about 100 individuals were found to be resident in the area during the winter months (when they could more easily be counted). Mammals added up to 10 species, including horses, dogs, cats and the commoners' cattle. The fallow deer were frequently observed. Reptiles numbered 3 species, so did amphibians, and there was a solitary fish in the brook, the three-spined stickleback. During this survey a number of invertebrate animals were recorded, but only three groups were given detailed attention. These were the dragonflies (15 spp), the day-flying lepidoptera (including the now extinct white admiral butterfly and holly blue), and 25 species of gall insects found on oak, willow and wild rose. A census in 1945 of the fungi, made with the assistance of the British Mycological Society, came to 76 species.

In 1947–8 a further study was made by the Chingford branch, this time on a number of sites where bombs had fallen during World War II. Nine such areas were selected. The clearing made by each explosion where trees had been blasted underwent a gradual regeneration to the former woodland condition. This took place in a definite succession. Firstly, there was a primary invasion on the ground by various herbaceous plants, including grasses, also a number of tree seedlings especially birch. Next, a birch-bramble thicket developed and eliminated the herb layer. Finally, with a closing in of the birch canopy, the bramble was suppressed, and only a few of the herbs, in particular grasses, persisted beneath the trees. This type of recolonisation by plants towards the original condition before the disturbance is a natural process which can be followed as an interesting object study for a naturalist. Similar ecological studies have been carried out by the author in the Forest, and two of these are described in Chapter 19.

A further group of naturalists comprises the Epping Forest Branch of the nationwide British Naturalists' Association, of which the author has the honour to be president. The association was founded in 1905 by E. Kay Robinson, a farsighted nature lover with particular regard for the preservation of the countryside and wildlife. At his own expense he published and sold (for only one penny) a weekly picture magazine of twenty-four pages, called *The Countryside*. Today this journal, now published half-yearly and running to some fifty pages, is regarded as one of the finest periodicals of its kind—a non-specialist publication about all aspects of wildlife and natural history activities in Britain, with contributions by its members and others, book reviews and news from its many branches. The founder, EKR, as he is known to BNA members, died in 1928, expressing a hope that his association and its journal would continue to flourish, and to follow the principle laid down in its motto: *Beatus est Naturae Amor*. This can be expressed in another way: 'To study and emjoy but not to kill.'

The Epping Forest Branch of the association was formed in 1937 as a successor to the Woodford branch of the LNHS, and carries on the normal activities of outdoor meetings, field surveys and indoor lectures. For a while after World War II the branch struck a bad patch. However, in 1960 a vigorous recruiting campaign and public meeting organised by Mrs Doreen Boardman, a local mycologist, resulted in an encouraging rise in membership, since which time the branch has not looked back. Through the generosity of Col Mallinson, of the White House, Woodford, the branch manages part of his estate as a nature reserve.

Such is a brief resumé of some of the naturalists of Epping Forest. Between them they have produced, mostly as amateurs in their spare time, an impressive store of knowledge about this historically famous British woodland. By such local efforts and the pride now taken in 'London's Forest', the wishes expressed by Gilbert White, in the passage which heads this chapter, are fully justified.

# 18

# GEOLOGY AND PREHISTORY

London and its neighbouring Forest lie in the midst of the Tertiary clays and sands which are overlain in places by later glacial gravels and boulder clay deposits. This clay covers the Thames basin, extending eastwards to Ipswich and Canterbury, and narrows inland towards Marlborough. Beyond this lies the familiar chalk of the downlands, forming ridges to the north and south of London. The Chiltern Hills cross Hertfordshire and Essex to the north, and the North Downs extend across Surrey and Kent to the south. This chalk is part of a folded system which dips deep below the London Basin. The later Tertiary deposits consist mainly of London Clay, and are much eroded in many places, but still of fair thickness in the London area. At Loughton a deep boring by the old Great Eastern Railway Company revealed a thickness of more than 200ft. Farther south it may reach 500ft in depth. This is the medium through which the Underground service carries its daily City commuters to and from the Forest district. When freshly exposed, this marine deposit has a slate-blue colour, but soon turns brown on weathering. London Clay was laid down in the Eocene Period, and is rich in marine fossils, principally of crustaceans and molluscs, shark's teeth and pieces of wood. These are best searched for after a cliff fall along the foreshore, at such places as Herne Bay and Sheppey. In the Forest itself there are no suitable exposures. Occasionally during building operations beds of oyster shells are uncovered, as happened during the erection of Harlow New Town and the Debden estate behind Loughton.

Much of the Forest clay has been eroded away or cut into by the streams, and may only be 30ft or less in thickness. Towards the surface it tends to become loamy and mixed with sand in places. This is especially so where the next bed occurs, called the Bagshot sands. This is widely spread over the Hampshire Basin, and around Aldershot and Bagshot where heaths are a common sight. In Essex it is thinly scattered between Epping and Ongar, and at Brentwood and Rayleigh. In the actual Forest there is only one place where it exists, at High Beech. This was discovered during the building of the small reservoir, and examined by the Essex Field Club. High Beech, some 500ft above sea-level, is close to the highest part of the Forest.

Above the Bagshot level, and of very much later date, are some patches of pebbles mixed with flint fragments, known as the Westleton Shingle. This can be seen at Jack's Hill, and also along the Earl's Path between Loughton and High Beech. These are of late Pliocene origin, and much earlier than the more widespread material of glacial origin laid down during the Ice Age or Pleistocene Period, and known as boulder clay. This is thought to have washed out of the melting glaciers and ice sheets, and spread over the landscape. It may contain fossils, such as belemnites from the Lias rocks to the north and ammonites from the Cretaceous. Stone fragments as well as chalk pebbles are common in the boulder clay, and may have been carried hundreds of miles in the moving ice sheets before they were released. This clay is fairly consistent and of a bluish grey to brown colouring. It occurs as far south as Chigwell beyond the Roding valley, and at Finchley west of the Lea. On the watershed in between it stops just north of Epping, and the Lower Forest lies on such clay. This may explain its damp and ofter waterlogged condition.

Farther south lie the beds of gravel formed through river action. These can be seen at the various gravel pits, now forming ponds, such as those on Wanstead and Leytonstone Flats. Successive invasions of the ice which spread down from the north caused a rise and lowering of sea-level, thereby affecting the rate of flow of the river Thames and its tributaries. During a warm interglacial, a rise in sea-level due to melting ice would have slowed up the river's flow, thus causing a widening of its flood-plain with a deposit of mud and gravel. Next, when a glacial phase occurred and the sea-level fell, the Thames would have cut a channel into its bed because of a faster flow, leaving behind a terrace of gravel along its upper slopes. In this manner successive levels of the river's former course can be seen today where gravel terraces exist at different heights above the present river. The oldest terrace is also the highest, and lies about 100ft above the present level. It comes just within the southern part of the Forest, at Wanstead.

Finally, along the banks of the Lea and Roding, and on the fields of the valley floors are the finer and more recent deposits of alluvium, a rich soil once used extensively along the two valleys by farmers and market gardeners, such as the tomato growers below Upshire.

In frequent excavations along the Lea Valley, especially during the building of the various reservoirs at Walthamstow, a section shows how the alluvial soil gives way to a more loamy clay, then sand and gravel, with the London Clay below it all at some 8–10ft depth. In the course of this work many interesting finds, both human and animal, have been made.

### PREHISTORIC FINDS

Most of the fossils found in the Epping Forest area are of a comparatively young date in geological timing. They have turned up during the various excavations carried out in the river and glacial deposits of the two bordering valley floors of the Lea and Roding. This puts them within the Pleistocene Period, popularly termed the great Ice Age.

One fertile locality was discovered among the various brick-fields at Ilford where, during the 1860s, Sir Antonio Brady made his fine collection of mammoth and other remains now among the national treasures in the Natural History Museum (see page 164). Apart from numerous mammoth bones and tusks, the

Ilford finds included red deer, bear, wolf, fox, lemming, musk-ox and reindeer, all of which still exist today, but more commonly in the Arctic. Among the now extinct species were the lion, hyena, wild horse, bison, aurochs, Irish deer, rhinoceros, hippopotamus and southern elephant. Some of these, notably the mammoth, roamed the Thames valley and over the present Forest ground during the cold or glacial phase of the Ice Age, whereas the hippopotamus occupied the river during a much warmer or interglacial period. Each species belonged to a warm or cold climate and is associated with certain races of prehistoric man whose remains, tools and other handiwork have been found in Western Europe and in Britain.

To understand this fluctuation in climates, animals and humans, one must consider the Ice Age not as a continuous state of extreme cold, but as a succession of ice invasions which moved south as a broad sheet to cover most of Britain on a number of separate occasions. These were the cold or glacial phases. In between, when ice melted and so retreated north, warmer inter-glacial phases took their place. During the last glacial, when ice reached a position just north of the Thames valley, there was dry land between Britain and Europe and the mammoth roamed the bleak tundra with Neanderthal man in pursuit. This rather brutish human with receding forehead, jutting eyebrows and prognathous jaws was eventually replaced by Cro-magnon man, our direct ancestor. His remains are known from Britain as well as Europe, and he is associated with more sophisticated handi-work in stone and bone. Perhaps his chief claim to fame is his skill as an artist. Paintings on the cave walls, notably at Lascaux in France, and Altamira in the Spanish Pyrenees, still exist after 10,000 years, and have been greatly admired by modern scholars.

Cro-magnon man followed the reindeer and fed on its meat, also that of wild horses and cattle. Quite possibly, like the Lap-lander today, he followed the migrating herds of deer, horse and bison as they moved back and forth with the seasons. The North Sea and Channel were then dry land, from the Channel Islands as far north as Yorkshire, and the famous fishing ground of the

Dogger Bank was a range of low-lying hills. Here he pursued the greatest quarry, the mammoth, setting pit-falls in which to trap it.

In his ceaseless search for fresh meat, man the hunter probably took good care to avoid too close a contact with the other hunters, such as lion, hyena, bear and wolf. One interesting thing did emerge, however. It is thought that a common bond sprang up between wolf and man as they pursued the same deer or other prey. Wolves gave chase and cornered the deer, and humans went in for the kill. Out of this was one day to appear the first of man's domestic helpmates—the dog.

These two Old Stone Age or Palaeolithic hunters, Neanderthal and Cro-magnon, were eventually replaced by the Mesolithic people who lived long after the bitter cold of the ice climate had ended. They settled in loosely knit communities on the banks of rivers and lakes, during a cool and relatively wet period in Britain. The finding of abundant harpoons carved out of deer antlers attest to their activities as fishermen. On parts of the Forest have been found minute flint objects, called microliths, which were used to tip their arrows, or fitted as barbs to their wooden spears. At a very much later stage, as history was already dawning in the Middle East, a farming folk of the Neolithic Period ferried across to Britain at a time when it was already cut off from the mainland. They settled and made their villages in clearings on the upland slopes of the drier and more fertile chalk to the north and south of the London Clay of the Thames basin. Here were the dense, wetter oakwoods which they tended to avoid, so that little is known of their presence in Epping Forest. A possible Neolithic trade route has been traced by Dr Rudge, the Wanstead antiquarian, which leads from the ancient flint mines at Grimes Graves on the Norfolk–Suffolk border, skirting the present Forest to the west, and ends at the town of St Albans. This was a Neolithic settlement long before the Romans turned it into a garrison town.

It is with the arrival of the metal workers of the Bronze and Iron Ages that we have ample evidence of occupation in the

Thames and Lea valleys bordering the Forest. Fruitful finds have turned up near Walthamstow during the construction of the reservoirs along the Lea valley. Spearheads, arrowheads and knives of bronze, and a sword, dagger sheath and pots of iron were among the finds made by the workmen. This at last brings us to the discovery and reconstruction of the earliest known Forest community—the Hallstadt people of the early Iron Age, who lived in pile dwellings on the Lea marshes and possibly built the Forest camps (see page 14). Associated with these finds were the remains of wolf, fox, wild boar, beaver, red and roe deer, and a small species of cattle, *Bos longifrons*. These are all modern animals of a much later date than those in the Ilford deposits mentioned above. Some useful references giving more detail of these prehistoric finds are listed in the Bibliography.

# 19

# ECOLOGY

Men that undertake only one district are much more likely to advance Natural Knowledge than those that grasp at more than they can possibly be acquainted with. Every kingdom, every province should have its own Monographer.

GILBERT WHITE of Selborne

During 2,000 years of human settlement most of Britain has undergone drastic changes at the hand of man. Even where the original woodland still exists, there is much artificiality caused by lopping and felling, grazing and hunting, as in the case of Epping Forest. Even so, there is much of scientific interest to be studied in such an area. Over the years as part of my training as a student, and in subsequent research, I have carried out a number of observations into plant growth and animal behaviour in what are ideal surroundings for field-work. This has been described in another book (see Bibliography). This present chapter is included in order to suggest to the reader how he or she, by quiet observation and with a little trouble and patience, can spend a while in the Forest to find out something about the fascinating way in which nature goes about her daily and nightly business.

It must quickly become obvious that no single species of plant or animal is entirely independent. Somehow and at some stage in its life, it must rely on the presence of another species, perhaps as a food, or as a means of shelter or protection. The study of the interrelation between living things in their home surroundings, is termed ecology (Greek, *oikos*: a house). This is fast becoming the modern method of biological instruction and research, by using the outdoors as a classroom or laboratory. Epping Forest, so close to London, is looked upon by many, not least of all the Forest Conservators, as a valuable territory for scientific study, and for use by serious naturalists. Steps have now been taken to provide facilities at a new centre within the Forest where such instruction and work can be carried out (see pages 198–9).

Because of its trees, Epping Forest represents a habitat called a woodland. This supports its own community of wildlife which is adapted to such surroundings. Of all the varied habitats found in Britain, the woodland community is perhaps one of the richest. It owes this to the dominant species, the trees themselves.

To a botanist, some of the most interesting parts of the Forest are the places where the trees have been removed, either by felling or a fire. It is here that one can witness the work of nature as she gradually fills up the gap—what is termed a 'biological vacuum'. One area studied by the author is the open glade on Long Running, just north of the Wake Arms crossroads (see page 44). Over the years this has slowly been developing into a birch wood, which is periodically checked by Forest fires here and there. An examination of any burnt patch the following season will probably reveal the presence of some primitive plants, the start of what is called a biosere. This is a series of plant growths which appear in succession over the years, leading ultimately to the 'climax' growth of trees, that is, a woodland. To begin with, one notices that the bare soil after rain is turning green as a film of lowly algae spreads over it. Later on, mosses and liverworts begin to appear, and perhaps a fern or two. These plants represent the flowerless groups, which reproduce by means of minute spores carried in the wind, and are usually the first to appear on bare places. Certain fungi, too, will turn up. This is called the Bryophyte stage in the biosere. Then, in a year or so, the seed plants begin to turn up. Prolific wind-borne seeds of grasses and rushes are among the first, and this becomes the grass or herb stage. It will include a number of plants with more showy flowers, the species depending on the nature of the soil.

At Long Running, which is acid, one can expect to find patches of heather, tormentil, heath bedstraw, speedwell and purple moor grass re-colonising the burnt area. They all occur locally. If the ground has been burnt, then the hair-moss, *Polytrichum*, and the rosebay are almost certain to appear, since both enjoy burnt places. As well as these herbs there may appear some species of more sturdy and woody growth, such as gorse and ling. These will form the shrub stage. Meanwhile, and possibly after the first year, numbers of tree seedlings will settle and germinate. On Long Running this is mainly birch, a rapid coloniser which tolerates the poorer soils. Slowly, as the young birches grow and gradually outreach all the other plants, a miniature woodland or tree stage is reached. All these stages—Bryophyte, grass, herb, shrub and tree—may be seen in a mature woodland. In Epping Forest this is best seen in the Lower Forest, where the oak and hornbeam form the tree canopy. Other places where beech dominates are a little disappointing, because of the paucity of undergrowth. As soon as the tree leaves have appeared by early summer, a heavy shade settles over the woodland. In a beech-wood as much as 80 per cent of daylight may be cut off. This limits the number of ground plants to those which can tolerate shade for much of the growing season, can store up a food reserve in organs such as bulbs and rhizomes, and usually blossom in the spring when light is still available. This brings to mind such flowers as the bluebell, anemone, primrose and wild arum. They are all adapted to woodland conditions (see Chapter 12).

Trees are precious. They dominate the scene and provide a canopy which shields the soil from the elements, and the roots bind it together. Without the trees the soil would soon dry out under the sun's rays. Wind and rain would blow and wash it away. In this manner, in places where man has felled a forest in the past, and put back nothing in its place, a man-made desert has resulted.

In addition to these protective measures, trees provide moisture and nourishment. A surprising amount of water is transpired from the tree leaves during the course of an hour.

Bearing this in mind one can understand the reason for the cool-
ness of a wood during a sultry summer's day, or the relative
warmth of the surroundings when a biting winter's gale is blowing outside. Nourishment comes from the annual fall of leaves
which forms continual layers of leaf-mould. This, so to speak, is
nature's compost heap, so valued by gardeners. In such surroundings life can be prolific, and hardly a square inch of soil is
wasted. The leaf-mould itself teems with life. This is the hidden
world of the litter fauna, a task force of worms, woodlice, spiders,
millepedes, grubs, and a host of other invertebrates, all busily
breaking up the fallen leaves and branches. Aided by those
agents of decay, the bacteria and fungi which can operate in the
dark, this army beneath our feet is preparing the food for the
woodland plants. This is nature's fertiliser, the mineral salts so
necessary to life.

Here is the start to a food-chain in the cycle of living. The
salts nourish the plants, which then supply animals with food,
some of whom in turn feed on their vegetarian neighbours. All
in time will die, so that each decaying leaf and carcass might give
back what was taken from the soil. The cycle is complete and, in
the steady flow of energy along the food-chains, it is important
that there should not be any gap or, even more important, any
serious competition. In a woodland each plant, being static,
takes up a certain position, usually at a certain height—the
lowly mosses at ground level, and the lofty trees at the top. Even
the root systems grow at different levels below ground. In this
manner woodland plants can grow close together, so much so
that it may be difficult to walk without treading on them.

Animals are more concerned with searching for food than
occupying a space. They each belong to a food 'niche', and live
according to where the food supply is to be had—below ground,
in a bush or tree, and so on. Here again, no two species will
normally occupy the same niche. The badger, a powerful digger
with strong legs and claws, builds its own underground fortress,
and grubs around for anything from worms to baby rabbits to
satisfy its catholic appetite. It has a keen sense of smell, but its

sight and hearing are indifferent. It has no need for speed, and no natural enemies. On the other hand, a timid ground-dweller like the rabbit is a speedy bundle of nerves, as it needs to be to avoid the keenness of fox and stoat on its trail. The squirrel can make for the trees as refuge, and there find much of its food out of harm's way (see diagram on page 82).

Woodland birds illustrate very clearly the share-out of space and food. The pheasant lives and nests on the ground, searching for food in the soil, as well as certain ground plants. The tiny warbler, during the time of the year when it visits us, nests in a low bush and hunts insects from trees. The finch chooses a thick bush in which to nest and seek out seeds and berries. The woodpecker has a tree for its home, larder, and drumming station; grubs and nuts are its food. A hollow tree makes a home for the tawny owl, whose tiny prey, the woodmouse and shrew, can be heard from above as they rustle through the leaf litter.

Food chains in which all the above take part can be likened to a pyramid. The energy flow from one stage to the next can be measured in terms of numbers and weight. For example, in woodland, countless numbers of leaves are eaten by a host of insects of about equal weight, such as certain caterpillars. These are eaten in turn by a lesser number of song birds, since each is much larger and heavier. In turn a certain number are preyed upon by a single pair of sparrow-hawks. At the base of this pyramid are the leaves which cover the woodland. On the leaves are the caterpillars, which hardly stray from one branch to the next. Then come the song birds occupying their separate territories within the wood. Finally, the sparrow-hawks have the entire wood to themselves. There is a definite relationship between size and living space, and the position held in the pyramid.

Since, in order to survive, a species must reproduce at a sufficient rate to maintain its numbers, it follows from the above that caterpillars must appear each season in vast numbers. Nothing like as many song birds are needed, although they may produce fair-sized families, even two or three clutches per year. On the other hand, the sparrow-hawk's annual family, a modest three or four babies, can expect to grow to adulthood and in time reproduce further generations. This is the food pyramid at work. It is when man interferes that things may go wrong. For centuries the sparrow-hawk has been trapped and shot as the enemy of the gamekeeper. This was bad enough, but today an even more deadly killing agent is at work. The present rarity of the hawk is almost certainly due to the widespread and often careless use of poison sprays in agriculture and weed clearance, though it should be stressed that no such sprays are used on the Forest. Right through the food pyramid the poisons become more and more concentrated, from leaves to caterpillars, through song birds and so to the final link in the chain, the so-called 'apex' species, in this case the bird of pray. For this unfortunate bird this has now become a pyramid of death, or at least infertility.

This kind of interrelationship between different animals and plants is but one example of the complicated food-web which operates in a woodland like Epping Forest, and shows how we can so easily, and perhaps thoughtlessly, cause harm. It is because of such places, like the Forest, which have been created for the enjoyment of people, first for hunting and then for pleasure, that we can come into close intimacy with nature. In such outdoor classrooms we can endeavour to learn more about the natural world around us, from which we stem. This is becoming more and more necessary as the human population rises and the invasion of rural areas spreads. To live with nature, to enjoy it, to conserve it and to hand it on to our descendents should be our aim. The conservators are fully aware of this, but how is the human tide to be controlled? To avoid the danger of losing all this Forest heritage, the warning given in the Epilogue to this book should be heeded in time—before it is too late.

# EPILOGUE—A DYING FOREST?

> The fault is great in man and woman,
> Who steals a goose from off a common.
> But what can plead that man's excuse,
> Who steals a common from a goose?
> anonymous letter to the *Tickler Magazine*
> (February 1821)

To many people the very word forest has an ominous ring to it
—a dark welter of trees and bushes with traps for the unwary,
such as dense undergrowth and muddy ditches to stumble into,
and no recognisable landmarks to follow. This is in marked contrast to the familar regimentation of street lighting, metalled
roadways, stone pavements and formal parks. This may be why
most urban dwellers shun the Forest depths, as their ancestors
once did. Most visitors still resort to the open spaces close to the
roadways, and ready access by means of rail and road bring out
thousands each weekend. Crowds can be found at places such as
Wanstead Flats, Chingford Plain and round the Forest inns at
High Beech, the Wake Arms and the Royal Forest Hotel.

Since World War II, however, there has been a noticeable
increase in the number of visitors and local residents who prefer
to penetrate the deeper recesses of the Forest. Ramblers,
naturalists and horse-riders are now in evidence on most days,
while a constant tide of traffic moves up and down the A11. This,
in the author's estimation, is the reason for a decline, even a loss,
of some of the Forest wildlife. With a growing awareness of its
attractions, and as a pleasant contrast to the monotony and drab-

ness which many Londoners must face in their daily lives, a visit to the Forest is understandable. Indeed, this is the very reason for its existence, as a place 'for use and enjoyment'. This is a splendid thing, but there is a growing danger which is becoming much of a world problem—the increase in humans. Today, man's major obstacle in trying to save the countryside and its wildlife, is man himself. Situated as it is on the fringe of the world's greatest metropolis, Epping Forest is bound to feel the impact.

People, of course, are welcome, and the majority are well behaved and come to the Forest for some harmless leisure activity. This could take the form of a ramble, horse-ride, picnic outing, or some more serious pastime, such as photography, painting, natural history or archaeology. Taken as individuals visitors make little impact, but in ever-increasing numbers their constant presence and disturbance must leave its mark. A party of bird-watchers can do more harm than a single poacher. To this must be added a certain amount of deliberate vandalism, such as tree damage, occasional fire raising, the carrying and use of firearms, even the collecting of natural history specimens. All these acts are contrary to the bye-laws. The gathering of pond-life, fungi, wild flowers, reptiles and small mammals by naturalists, is no doubt in a good cause, but is still an offence. The study of nature and the pursuit of knowledge is commendable, but carried out in this manner 'in the field' year after year is bound to have its effect. Wildlife, although resilient to pressure and competition, can only take so much, then it retreats.

In the long run it is the sheer pressure of human presence which must disturb the Forest's wildlife. This is now becoming a nationwide problem in all those places which have been set aside for recreation and the enjoyment of natural beauty, such as the regional parks, National Trust property, and similar places open to the public. There is a sad irony in this situation, in that the very purpose for which these open spaces were created is defeating its own end.

So far Epping Forest has suffered some loss of wildlife, but to date it has resisted all encroachment of any significance, due to the vigilance of its conservators. Apart from some road widening and the erection of some necessary buildings, the Forest still remains unenclosed, free and open to all. How long can this last? How long will it withstand the demand for more housing space, extra roads, shops, schools and hospitals, and for all the other needs of a growing community?

People's needs, they say, must come first, but there is now a growing awareness that there is more to this than just the physical demands. Man also has a spiritual and mental appetite which needs to be fed, especially among those who live in built-up areas. A kind of sickness can arise among those who grow up in an atmosphere of noise, artificiality and pollution, and are starved of what our ancestors have experienced for thousands of years—the good earth, the green pastures and the overhanging trees. To many the rural landscape of Britain is something precious which must be preserved. Today the scene of sheep grazing over the Yorkshire moors and Kentish marshlands, or the cattle wandering over Dartmoor and through Epping Forest, is much the same as it was 2,000 years ago. In this we see the manifestation of a pastoral practice as old as farming itself, a birthright handed down from our Neolithic ancestors. Neolithic, Bronze Age, Celtic, Saxon and English, all these farmers and herdsmen have practised and handed on the right to own land and work on it. By what right have we, in a single century, to take away these places and liberties with our spreading roads, reservoirs, aerodromes and bingo halls? The manner of ceding commonland to particular private owners and manors, as in the case of Epping Forest, dates back to as early as the ninth century. But, and it is an important 'but', the land has to remain open to the people. The bitter fight of the last century against the eighteen lords of the manors, for once victorious, is the great event in our Forest story.

It is to be hoped that the royal commission on common land will ensure a proper legislation to bring about statutory registration of all such land and its common rights so that some of our realm at least may remain free and open for all to enjoy. For, once the common right is lost, the land may go with it. Should Epping Forest, in spite of all it means to the Londoner, still be unable to resist the demands of a growing populace, then it may one day become engulfed in a human flood, never to return. A precious plot of England will be lost for ever.

# THE LANGUAGE OF THE
# FOREST: A GLOSSARY

England, the home of a nation of mixed ancestry, has a language second to none. Its variety and richness is due to the many tongues which have been spoken between these shores in bygone days. As each invader came and went, or was absorbed into the community, a further set of words was added to the mother tongue. In this manner a remarkable store of foreign words has been handed down to the present day. Many such words, whose meaning and pronunciation can baffle even a native, are inherent in the common speech of the huntsman, forester, lawyer and landlord; this is particularly true of the great hunting era, from the Normans to the Stuarts, as described in this book. These words from the past may sound strange and archaic to modern ears, yet their roots go deep into the countryside. It would be a great pity to see them die out altogether.

### TERMS IN FOREST LAW

AFFOREST  To convert into forest or hunting ground. To place under forest law (see Forest).

AGIST (O. French *agister*—to lodge)  To take in livestock to remain and feed in a special place. To admit cattle on to the forest for a definite period.

AGISTER  The forest official who controls the pasturing of cattle on forest land.

AMERCE (Anglo-French *amercier*)   Originally a gift or remuneration offered as a recompense. Later treated as a fine, hence 'to be amerced' or 'in mercy' to someone for the amount of the fine, ie the penalty was left to the mercy of the inflictor.

BAILIFF (Latin *bajulivus*—a carrier)   A carrier-on or administrator. A person charged with public administration and originally so authorised by the Crown, eg a sheriff, mayor or some king's officer, especially the chief officer of a Hundred (which see); a bailiff of a waterway, castle, etc.

BAILIWICK   The district or place under the jurisdiction of a bailiff (which see). The bailiwick town was the chief town of a Hundred (which see).

BOOKLAND (O. English *boc*—a book)   Taken from the folcland (folkland) or common land, and granted by the *boc* or written charter to some private owner; thus eventually applied to all land which was not common land (see also Charter).

BRASH (possibly derived from French *brèche*—a heap of broken stone, hence the Italian *breccia*. Also meaning the refuse of boughs, branches, twigs and hedge clippings)   Brashwood, the lower side branches removed by foresters from young conifers at a certain age.

BROWSE (16th-cent. French *broust*—a young shoot)   Also applied to the fodder for cattle, etc. The 'browse or meate for beastes in snowtyme'—Hulvel, 1552. Also, 'The Foresters must provide Browsewood to bee cut down for (the Deer) to feed upon'—Manwood, *Lawes Forrest*, 1615.

BROWSER   One who feeds the deer (in wintertime).

CHARTER (O. French *chartre*, from Latin *cartula*—a small paper or writing)   A legal document usually written on a single sheet of parchment, by which grants, contracts and cessions were ratified; a written document delivered by the sovereign, such as the Forest Charter, or Carta de Foresta (*carta*, Latin for paper).

COMMON (Latin *com*—together, and *munis*—bound under obligation)   Land of a general, public or non-private nature; in forest law applied to undivided land belonging to members of a local community as a whole; a patch of unenclosed or 'waste' land.

The ancient 'right of common' or common right was and still is the advantage or profit which a person has in the land or water belonging to another. Examples are the common of pasture (pasturing cattle), common of estovers (gathering firewood), common of turbary (cutting turf), common of piscary (fishing), and common of agistry (feeding pigs) etc (which all see).

COMMONALTY (Latin *communalitas*) A free and self-governing community.

COMMONER (see Common) One who has a joint right on common lands.

COPPICE. Also copse (Latin *colpaticium*—having the quality of being cut. O. French *copeiz*) A small wood or thicket consisting of underwood and small trees grown for the purpose of periodical cutting. Coppice wood—underwood. Coppicing—the cutting down of trees or shrubs at ground level, as opposed to pollarding (which see).

CURTILAGE (Med. Latin *curtilagium*—a small court or garth) The courtyard or garth, ie the piece of land attached to a dwelling house and forming one enclosure with it.

DEMESNE (Anglo-French *demeyne*, later *demesne*) Possibly derived from domain (Latin *dominicum*). Belonging to a lord, seigneurial or dominal; the nature of private land, ie real estate in law.

DISAFFOREST The removal of land from forest law (see Forest).

ESTOVER (O. French *estovour*—to be necessary) A necessity allowed by law, especially the wood which a tenant is permitted to gather from his landlord's estate for the purpose of repairing his home, hedge, cart, implements, etc. Also, a kind of alimony for a widow or a woman separated from her husband. On forest land there once existed a right of common of estover.

EYRE (O. French *eire*; Latin *iterare*—to journey) The circuit court. The Justice in Eyre was the itinerant judge who visited the various forest courts.

FEE (O. English *feoh*; Dutch *vee*—cattle) Livestock such as cattle, horses, pigs, etc. Deer were called wild fee. Feudal law refers to property, livestock or deer which were held on condition of homage or service to a superior lord, by whom it was granted and in whom the ownership remained. Fee deer were offered by the Crown to visiting dignitaries as a gift for the pleasure of hunting. A fief was a feudal benefit.

FOREST (O. French *foris*—outside or without) The word is taken out of its old legal context in the Latin phrase '*forestem silvam*' (*silva*—Latin for wood). A forest is thus the 'outside wood', or land beyond the walls of a closed-in park or estate, and subject to the special forest law which safeguarded the deer and trees (see Vert and Venison).

GREENHUE (Danish *hueg*—to strike or deal a blow) The green parts in woods and forests, synonymous with the Norman-French *vert* (which see).

HAIE (O. French, an obsolete form of hay, derived from O. English *haga*—a hedge; as in hawthorn, the 'hedge' thorn) Norman barons, jealous of their rights to land, and fearing the loss of game, introduced a system of dividing this into parks and hays (haiae). The latter were small enclosures for herding deer. Domesday Book lists 31 parks and more than 70 hays. The royal parks in London, such as Hyde Park and St James's Park, were used by James I for the harbouring of fallow deer, and there is a record of deer stealers being caught and executed at the park gates. Deer remained in these two parks until their removal at the coronation of Queen Victoria.

HEYNING (M. English *hain*, from the Norse) An enclosure or park. A winter heyning was an enclosure for holding cattle during the winter period; a grassy preserve for feeding animals.

HOCKSINEW (*Hock*, origin uncertain—a joint in the hindleg of a quadruped between the knee and fetlock or ankle) To disable by severing the tendon of the ham or hock, in man or beast; to hamstring.

HUNDRED   The decimal unit; the cardinal number equal to five score or ten times ten. In England (later in Ireland) a sub-division since medieval times of a county or shire having its own court. Said to be an area capable of supporting a hundred families or hides, also an area which could supply a hundred fighting men for the defence of the realm, eg the Becontree Hundred, the Havering Hundred, etc.

KINDLING (O. Norse *kyndill*—a candle or torch)   Referring to combustible matter, such as firewood or brush used to start a fire. From which—to kindle, meaning to excite, stir up or inflame.

LAMMAS (O. English *hlafmoesse*; *hlaf*—bread and *moesse*—mass)   1 August, observed in the early English church as a festival where loaves of bread were consecrated and made from the first ripening corn.

LAWED (O. Norse *lagu*—something laid down or fixed)   Provided with laws; subject to a rule or conduct fixed by the community. Thus, dogs, cattle and other domestic animals were 'lawed' if allowed on to forest soils, and subject to the Lawes Forrest.

LIBERTY (Latin *liber*—free)   In law, a privilege or exceptional right granted to a subject or community by the sovereign. In England before 1850 this applied to a district within the limits of a county which was exempt from the jurisdiction of the county sheriff, and held a separate commission of the peace (see the Liberty of Havering, page 28); also a large district comprising several manors held by a single lord in whom was vested by grant or long usage the complete jurisdiction of the area.

LOPPING (O. English lop; Norwegian *loppa*—to pluck or snatch)   The removal by cutting, of branches and twigs from a tree; the cutting or removal of the extremities of a human body, such as head and limbs.

LORD (O. English *hlaford*—head of a household)   This word has many uses, such as a divinity, a person of high rank, even a husband; also the proprietor of a manor or fee who was originally some feudal superior, and called the lord of the manor.

MANOR (O. French *manoir*—a dwelling or habitation. Latin *manere*—to remain) The mansion or principal house of an estate; also, a unit of territorial ownership existing in feudal times from the tenth century; freehold land held in demesne (which see) by the lord, and including those lands occupied by tenants from whom the lord had the right to extract fines or fees, and over which land he held certain privileges, eg hunting rights.

MESSUAGE (O. French *masuage*—a tenement; Latin *mansuanus*) The portion of land occupied as a site for a dwelling house and its outbuildings, including the land assigned to its use, eg a garden, allotment, paddock etc (see also Curtilage).

MOOT (O. English *mot*—a meeting or assembly) Hence the moot hall, moot bell, moot book, moot court, etc.

PANNAGE (O. French *pasnage* 1272; Latin *pascere*—to feed) The old commoners' right to feed his swine on forest soil (for acorns).

PERAMBULATION (Latin *perambulatio*—the action of walking through; a journey or tour) The ancient ceremony of walking officially around the forest boundaries, or of a manor or parish, so as to fix the limits and to preserve the rights of possession or of hunting.

PISCARY (Latin *piscarius*—belonging to fishing) An old commoners' right to catch fish.

POLLARD (M. English and L. German *poll*—the head of man or beast) Used here in the sense of cutting or lopping the top or 'head' of a tree, some 6ft from the ground, ie the height of a man and his axe.

POUND (M. English *pund*—a fold) An enclosure maintained by authority for the detention of stray or trespassing cattle, and for their detention until redeemed by the owner; a pinfold. The word may also be derived from O. English *pynd*—to shut up of dam (water),eg the Pen Ponds in Richmond Park.

POURALLE (O. French *per*—through, and *alée*—going, derived from Latin *perambulatio,* ie a perambulation, which see) The land which was once under forest law, then was disafforested and so given back into private ownership and legally 'out of bounds' to the Crown.

REEVE (O. English *gerefa*) A high official having local jurisdiction under the king; the chief magistrate of a town, also a bailiff or steward; a forest official who supervised the movement and marking of the commoners' cattle and horses.

REGARD (Med. Latin *regardum*—aspect or appearance) The official inspection of a forest in order to discover whether any trespass had been committed (see page 77).

SALTARY (Latin *saltare*—to leap) A deer-leap over which a deer could leap and so enter an enclosed area, but could not leap out again. This was contrary to forest law. 'Neither may any man make any saltaries or leaping places out of the Forrest into the Pouralles, where anie Deere may easily leape in, but cannot return back again.' Manwood in *Lawes Forrest*, 1598. (See also Pouralle.)

SELECT PLEAS A specially chosen action which relates to the enforcement of forest law.

SWAINMOTE (O. Norman *sveinn*—a boy or servant; O. English *swan*) In its general meaning, a servant or attendant to some official, eg a coxswain, boatswain etc; a swain was also a freeholder serving on the jury of the forest court, or swainmote, ie meeting of the swains. (See also Moot.) 'This word Swaine in the Saxon spelling is a Bookeland man, which at this day is taken for a Charterar or a freeholder; and so the Swainmote is in English a Court within the Forest, whereunto all the freeholders doe owe suit and service'—Manwood.

STEW (French *estuir*—to shut up or keep in reserve) A pond or tank for keeping fish until required for the table; a stew-pond.

TURBARY (Latin *turbaria*; O. French (1200) *tourbe*; modern turf) An old commoners' right to gather peat or bracken as fodder or bedding for his animals, or as fuel.

VERDERER (variant of French *vert*—green) A forest official who keeps law and order. 'A judicial officer of the King's forest . . .

sworn to keep and maintain the assizes of the Forest, and also to view, receive and enrol the attachments and presentiments of all manner of trespass of the forest, of vert and of venison' —Manwood.

VENISON (O. French *veneson*; Latin venare—to hunt) The flesh of an animal killed in the chase or hunt, and used as food. Once applied to the flesh of deer, boar, rabbit, hare and other game, now only to deer meat. Venery—the sport or practice of chasing deer.

VERT (French *vert*, from Latin *viridis*—green) Applied to the green vegetation growing in a wood or forest, and serving as cover and food for deer. Is usually coupled with the word 'venison' (for deer) as being the two most important ingredients of a forest (see Venison). 'There are two sorts of Vert in every Forrest, that is to say, Ouer vert and Neather vert; Ouer vert is that which the Lawiers do call Hault Boys [ie *bois*—wood], and Nether vert is what the Lawiers do call South Boys, and in the Forrest Lawes Ouer vert is all manner of Hault Boys, or great wood, as well such as beareth fruit. Special vert is every tree that doth beare fruite to feed the Deere withal, as Pear trees, Crabtrees, Hawthorne, and such like'—Manwood.

VILL (Latin *vicus*—a village or hamlet) Also in part a villa, country house or farm; today, a village.

VILLEIN (Anglo-French *villein*) A serf under the feudal system; a peasant attached to a manor and subject to the lord; a serf or bondman, also applied at times to a rustic, labourer or person of low birth. Later corrupted to villain.

WOODWARD (O. English *wuduweard*) The keeper of the wood; the officer of wood or forest having charge of the growing and cutting of timber.

# BIBLIOGRAPHY

BOOKS ON EPPING FOREST AND LOCALITY

Addison, W. *Epping Forest, its historic and literary associations* (1946)

Brimble, J. A. *London's Epping Forest* (1950, also a later ed with colour), a pictorial extravaganza

Buxton, E. N. *Epping Forest* (1884 et seq), gives a sound historical summary

Fisher, W. R. *The Forest of Essex* (1887), exhaustive historical and legal detail

Leutscher, Alfred. *Field Natural History* (1969), includes many field studies carried out in the Forest

Lysons, Daniel. *Environs of London* (1796), vol 4

Neale, K. J. 'Queen Elizabeth's Hunting Lodge', *Bulletin No 3*, Chingford Historical Society (1965)

Ogbourne, Elizabeth. *History of Essex* (1810)

Perceval, P. J. S. *London's Forest* (1909), a picturesque and romantic account

Qvist, Alfred, Forest Superintendent. *Epping Forest* (Corporation of London, 1972)

Speakman, Fred. *A Poacher's Tale* (1960), country life in the Forest area

——. *A Keeper's Tale* (1961), as above

——. *A Forest by Night* (1963), an intimate and moving story

# Bibliography

## BOOKS ON HUNTING

Belany, J. C. *A Treatise upon Falconry* (1841)
Berners, Dame Juliana. *The Book of St Albans* (1486)
Daniel, the Rev B. J. *Rural Sports* (1801)
Hare, C. E. *The Language of Sport* (1925)
Leutscher, Alfred. *Tracks and Signs of British Animals* (1960)
Parker, Eric. *Game Pye* (1925)
Pye, H. J. *The Sportsman's Dictionary* (1807)
Turberville, G. *The Noble Art of Venerie* (1576)

## BOOKS ON ANIMAL LIFE

Cadman, W. A. *Roe Deer and Fallow Deer* (HMSO)
Clegg, John. *Freshwater Life of the British Isles* (1965)
Crystal, R. N. *Insects of British Woodlands* (1937)
Ford, E. B. *Moths* (1955)
——. *Butterflies* (1957)
Imms, A. *Insect Natural History* (1947)
Matthews, L. Harrison. *British Mammals* (1952)
Neal, Ernest. *The Badger* (1952)
Page, F. Taylor. *Field Guide to the British Deer* (Mammal Society, 1959)
Peterson, R. T. *Field Guide to the Birds of Britain and Europe*
Shorten, Monica. *Squirrels* (1948)
Smith, Malcolm. *British Amphibians and Reptiles* (1954)
Southern, N. (ed). *Handbook of British Mammals* (Mammal Society, 1964)
Whitehead, Kenneth. *The Deer of Great Britain and Ireland* (1964)

## BOOKS ON PLANT LIFE

Edlin, H. L. *Trees, Woods and Man* (1956)
Hadfield, Miles. *British Trees* (1957)
Jewell, A. *The Observer's Book of Mosses and Liverworts* (1955)

Kershaw, K. and Alvin, K. *The Observer's Book of Lichens* (1963)

Lange, M. and Hora, F. *Collins' Guide to Mushrooms and Toadstools* (1963)

McClintock, D. and Fitter, R. *Collins' Pocket Guide to Wildflowers* (1956)

Meldris, A. and Bangerter, E. *A Handbook of British Flowering Plants* (1955)

Step, E. *Wayside and Woodland Ferns—a Guide to the British Ferns, Horsetails and Clubmosses* (1945)

Wakefield, E. *The Observer's Book of Common Fungi* (1954)


ARTICLES PUBLISHED BY THE ESSEX FIELD CLUB

From the *Essex Naturalist*


DEER

Chapman, R. and D. 'A Preliminary Report on Some Fallow Deer (*Dama dama*) from Epping Forest', vol 31 pt 2 (1963)

Harting, J. 'The Deer of Epping Forest' (1887)


FLOWERS

Lister, Giulielma. 'Flora of Wanstead Park', vol 27 pt 4 (1941)

——. 'Additions to List of Flowering Plants in Wanstead Park', vol 27 pt 12 (1946)

Ross, Joseph. 'Some Interesting Plants of Epping Forest', vol 27 pt 5 (1942)


FOSSILS AND HISTORY

Marshall, Kenneth. 'Excavation of a Mesolithic Site near High Beach', vol 30 pt 3 (1959)

Smith, W. G. 'Primaeval Man in the Valley of the Lea' (trans Essex Field Club) vol 3 (1883)

Ward, Bernard. 'Some Essex Naturalists', vol 29 pt 5 (1936)

Warren, S. Hazzeldene. 'The Drifts of South-western Essex', vol 28 pt 5 (1942) & pt 6 (1943)

Woodward, H. 'The Ancient Fauna of Essex' (trans Essex Field Club, vol 3 (1883)

FUNGI

Boardman, Doreen. 'Earthstars in Epping Forest', vol 31 pt 2 (1963)
——. 'Fungi of Epping Forest—Basidiomycetes', vol 32 pt 4 (1970)
Lister, Giulielma. 'Mycetozoa, a Monograph' (1918)
Ross, Joseph. 'Mycetozoa—Records for Epping Forest', vol 27 pt 1 (1940) and pt 3 (1941); vol 28 pt 1 (1947, pt 2 (1948), pt 3 (1949), pt 4 (1950) and pt 5 (1951)
Ward, Bernard. 'Fungi of Epping Forest—Myxomycetes', vol 32 pt 5 (1971)
Wilberforce, Peter. 'Fungi of Epping Forest—Ascomycetes', vol 32 pt 4 (1970)

GALLS

Ross, Joseph. 'Oak Galls in Epping Forest', vol 28 pt 1 (1947)

LICHENS

Crombie, Rev J. 'On the Lichen Flora of Epping Forest and the Causes Affecting its Recent Diminution' (trans Essex Field Club, vol 14 pt 1 (1885), 170 species

MOSSES

Pettifer, A. J. 'A Bryophyte Flora of Essex' (1968)

REPTILES AND AMPHIBIANS

Malenoir, G. 'Further Notes on the Reptiles and Amphibians Survey of Epping Forest 1959–61', vol 31 pt 2 (1963)
——. 'Herpetological Notes', vol 32 pt 2 (1968)
Malenoir, G. and Pickett, J. 'A Survey of Adders in an Area in Epping Forest', vol 32 pt 2 (1968)
Wheeler, A., Malenoir, G. and Davidson, J. 'Survey of the

# Bibliography

Reptiles and Amphibians in Epping Forest', vol 30 (1959), and vol 31 (1963)

TREES
Elliott, F. W. 'Epping Forest Trees and Shrubs' (1898)
Paulson, R. 'Birch Groves in Epping Forest' (presidential address), vol 20 pt 2 (1922)

ARTICLES PUBLISHED BY THE LONDON NATURAL HISTORY SOCIETY
From the *London Naturalist*

BIRDS
*London Bird Report* (issued annually since 1916)

BUTTERFLIES
Worms, de, C. G. M. 'The Butterflies of London and its surroundings', No 62 (1949)

DRAGONFLIES
Pinniger, E. B. 'Notes on the Dragonflies of Epping Forest' (1932), 22 species
——. 'Epping Forest Odonata' (1933)

ECOLOGY
'Survey by the Chingford Branch of the LNHS 1941–48' (includes a history, mammals, birds, fungi, galls, hornets, bomb craters, climate)

FERNS
Payne, R. M. 'The Ferns of Epping Forest', No 39 (1959), 19 species

FLOWERS
Robbins, R. W. 'The Flora of Epping Forest' (1915)
Ross, J. 'Flora of Epping Forest' (1942)

# Bibliography

GREY SQUIRREL

Bevan, G. 'The Distribution of the Grey Squirrel in the London area (1953–6)', No 36 (1956)

Johnson, F. J. 'The Grey Squirrel in Epping Forest' (1937)

HISTORY

Simpson, A. L. 'The Story of Our Commons and a Chapter on the Essex Forests' (1934)

LIVERWORTS

Ross, J. 'The Hepatics Found in Epping Forest' (1924), 26 species

MYCETOZOA

Ross, J. 'Mycetozoa in Epping Forest', No 25 (1945), 106 species

POND PLANTS

Selby, C. H. 'Some Aspects of Dispersal and Succession of Plants in Some Epping Forest Ponds', No 34 (1954)

The *Essex Naturalist* and the *London Naturalist* are available for inspection at the British Museum (Natural History), Cromwell Rd, London, SW7, or possibly through a public library.

## SOCIETIES, FIELD COURSES AND MUSEUMS IN THE FOREST AREA

British Naturalists' Association (Epping Forest Branch). For address apply to author.

Chingford Historical, Wanstead and Woodford Historical and other similar local historical societies. For address inquire at local library.

Commons, Open Spaces and Footpaths Preservation Society, 166 Shaftesbury Avenue, London, WC2.

The Conservation Centre, High Beach. The City Corporation acting as Conservators of Epping Forest have built a centre which was opened on 23 June 1971 by HRH the late Prince William of Gloucester. It has a warden and resident staff, and is available to visitors and societies, also school parties, primarily as an educational centre with conservation in mind. It is operated by the Field Studies Council.

The Conservation Corps c/o Council for Nature. A voluntary service of young people willing to assist in conservation activities.

The Council for Nature c/o Zoological Society of London, NW1. A national clearing house and source of information on matters of natural history.

Debden Further Education Centre, Debden, Loughton. Residential courses, including subjects on natural history. Run by Newham Greater London Council.

Essex County Naturalists' Trust. Apply to main headquarters: Manor House, Alford, Lincs.

Essex Field Club. Headquarters at Passmore Edwards Museum, Romford Rd, Stratford E15.

Field Studies Council, 9 Devereux Court, London, WC2, runs a number of field centres for research purposes, and where residential courses are held for adults and senior school children.

London Natural History Society. For address apply to British Museum (Natural History), Cromwell Rd, London, SW7.

Passmore Edwards Museum, Romford Rd, Stratford E15.

Queen Elizabeth's Hunting Lodge, Chingford, Essex.

Suntrap Field Centre. A day centre for visiting school parties. Maintained by Waltham Forest Educational Committee.

Wansfell, Theydon Bois, Further Education Centre. Residential courses, including subjects on natural history. Run by Essex County Council.

# ACKNOWLEDGEMENTS

A book of this nature, the summation of a lifetime experience, and covering a wide expanse of time and subject matter, cannot be entirely free of errors. It has been written mainly as yet another reminder of a precious heritage we in Britain owe to our forbears who, with farsighted wisdom, anticipated the essential needs for the preservation of the dwindling open spaces within our crowded community.

I have endeavoured to tell this Forest story with the help of documented records mentioned in the Bibliography, as well as recounting something about the wildlife based on my own researches. More so than ever today is it necessary to be vigilant in safeguarding such countryside, not only for our own pleasure, but for the future of our wildlife and our children.

I wish especially to thank Bernard Ward, verderer of Epping Forest, for his kind advice on reading through the manuscript, also James Brimble, Geoffrey Kinns and the late Lionel Day for the use of their photographs. Many friends in natural history and historical circles, perhaps unknowingly, have given support and encouragement over the many years I have come to know and love this ancient woodland, the last remnant of the most favoured of the Kinge's Forrests.

Wanstead, Essex                                             Alfred Leutscher

# INDEX

*Page numbers in italic indicate illustrations*

Index

Norman kings, 28
Nuthatch, 109

Oak trees, 148
Office of Works, 34, 39
Owl, tawny, 109

Perambulation, 30–2
Pigs, 74–5
*Plantae Woodfordiensis*, 132, 136, 148, 161, 163
Poaching, 51, 60
Pond life, 156–9
Ponds, 45, 47, 115–16, *140*
Prehistoric life, 171
Prehistoric man, 172–4
Primroses, 133

Queen Elizabeth's Hunting Lodge, 47, 64, 159, 165

Rabbits, 59, 103
Ray, John, 163
Redbacked shrike, 114
Redpoll, 111
Redstart, 113
Redwing, 115
Regard, 77
Regeneration, 82, 167, 176
Reptiles, 45
Reservoirs, 154–5
Right of lopwood, 77–8
Rivers, Lea and Roding, 116, 128, 153, 157, 170, 171
Romans, 16

Saxon farming, 19
Saxon huntsman, 21
Saxon kings, 20
Select Pleas, 25, 50, 53
Sheep, 74
Shrews, 106
Siskin, 111
Skylark, 114
Sparrow-hawk, 110, 179–80
Spotted flycatcher, 112
Stag beetles, 123

Stinkhorn, *140*
Stoats, 103
Stonechat, 114
Squirrel, grey, 88, 105
Squirrel, red, 105
Superintendent, 80
Swainmote, 52, 62

Thrushes, 112, 115
Tiger beetle, 119
Tits, 111
Toadstools, 144–7
Tree creeper, 109
Tree pipit, 113
Trees, 148–52
Trespass, 53
Truffle, 147
Turner, William, 134
Turpin, Dick, 34

Vanessid butterflies, 127
Vert and venison, 23
Victoria, Queen, 42, 43
Voles, 104

Waltham Forest, 20, 23, 28, 32
Walton, Izaak, 153, 154
Wanstead Park, 47, 103, 111, 112, 133, 142, 163
Warblers, 112
Warner, Richard, 134, 160
Water birds, 115
Waxwing, 112
Weasel, 103
Weevils, 123
Wheatear, 115
White, Gilbert, 160
Willingale, Tom, 39
Wimbledon Common, 38
Wood ant, 124
Woodcock, 111
Woodland ecology, 176
Woodmouse, 103
Woodpeckers, 108
Woodpigeon, 110
Wood wasp, 125
Wryneck, 109